International Accl

Commentary on the Forty

MW01285694

"I had the honor of reviewing Imam Didmar Faja's commentary on the classical *40 Hadiths* of Imam Al-Nawawi. It is a rich book with valuable insights and reminders. May Allah accept this work and bless us all through the teachings of the Prophet, peace be upon him."

—**Muhammad bin Yahya al-Ninowy**, author of *The Book of Love*

"I had the honor and pleasure of reading Imam Didmar Faja's meticulous study of the famous 'Forty Hadith' by Imam Al Nawawi. This comprehensive analysis not only deepens understanding but also enriches one's spiritual journey. I highly recommend this enlightening and useful work for anyone seeking profound insights into the teachings of Islam."

—**Burhan AlDin Fili**, author of *Hope is Alive*

"Mufti Faja's *Commentary on the Forty Hadiths of Imam Al-Nawawī* is a refreshing and insightful exploration of one of the most beloved collections of Prophetic traditions. With clarity and depth, Faja navigates the timeless wisdom of these hadiths, offering readers both spiritual reflection and practical guidance for everyday life. His approach makes this work accessible to both newcomers and seasoned students of Islamic knowledge. A must-read for anyone seeking to deepen their understanding of the Prophet's teachings."

—**Flamur Vehapi**, author of *Peace and Conflict Resolution in Islam*

"Imam Didmar Faja's *Commentary on the Forty Hadiths of Imam Al-Nawawī* is a timeless, necessary, rich, and beautiful work that is a must-read in our times. Utilizing accessible language and providing us with a comprehensive view into the classical 40 Hadiths of Imam Al Nawawi, Imam Didmar takes us on a beautiful and practical journey to reviving within each of our hearts, a deep love and connection to Prophet Muhammad (ﷺ) and his teachings. I highly recommend this book to anyone who is seeking to increase their love for the prophet (ﷺ), strengthen their ibadah (worship), and beautify their hearts with the sweetness of iman (faith)."

— **Marwa Assar**, author of *The Compass HOME*

بسم الله الرحمن الرحيم

In the Name of God, Most Gracious, Most Merciful
& Peace and Blessings Be Upon His Beloved ﷺ

ECHOES OF THE PROPHET
A COMMENTARY ON THE NAWAWI`S 40 HADITH

by
Imam Didmar Faja

First Published in English in 2024

The original book in Albanian was completed
with the help of God on 27 Muharram, 1436,
corresponding to 20 November, 2014,
while the translation was completed on 1 Muharram, 1446,
corresponding to 8 July, 2024, in Glendale, Arizona USA.

Paperback
ISBN: 978-1-300-90558-5

Library of Congress Control Number: 2024922942

Subjects:
Islam| Hadith | Sayings
Wisdom | Inspirations | Muslim
Nawawi

Text copy edited by Stella Williams.
Book designed and typeset by Elipse Productions.

First Published in the United States of America

Table of Contents

Preface by Imam Muhamed Sytari, Mufti of Shkodër, Albania[1]

"Forty Hadiths of Imam al-Nawawī's collection is a beloved and eagerly anticipated work among Albanian Muslims."

The distinguished compilation by Abū Zakariyyā Yaḥyā Ibn Sharaf al-Nawawī (died in 676 Hijri/1277 CE)[2] is widely recognized and accepted throughout the Muslim world. The enduring interest of Islamic scholars across centuries in elucidating this extensive work underscores its profound significance. The book's invaluable content resonates deeply in our daily lives.

The Forty Hadiths gained such renown that many sought to commit them to memory, driven by Imam al-Nawawī's sincere intention in compiling them, which Allah blessed by enabling millions to memorize them. Numerous eminent scholars have dedicated themselves to expounding upon the Forty Hadiths, resulting in approximately fifty commentaries in Arabic, some published and others preserved in manuscripts.[3]

---

[1] This is the Preface to the original book in Albanian.

[2] The Hijri date reflects the Islamic calendar, corresponding to the year in which the individual passed away, followed by the equivalent date in the Common Era (CE) calendar.

[3] Dr. Mustafa Al-Bugha and Muhyiddin Misto, *Al-Vafi fi Sharh al-Arbain Al-Nawawiyyah*, Damascus, no publishing year available, pg 5.

In their examination of Ibn Ḥajar al-ʿAsqalānī's (d. 852 H./1449) commentary on the Forty Hadiths, scholars like Riyāḍ Īsā al-Mansī and ʿAbdul Qādir Muṣṭafā Tāhā recognize the immense scholarly attention bestowed upon Imam al-Nawawī's work. They highlight several enduring commentaries, including:

- *Sharḥ al-Arbaʿīn Hadīthan al-Nawawiyyah* by Imam al-Nawawī (d. 676 H./1277)
- *Al-Tajīn fī Sharḥ al-Arbaʿīn* by Imam Tūfī (d. 716 H.)
- *Al-Manhaj al-Mubīn fī Sharḥ al-Arbaʿīn al-Nawawiyyah* by Imam Fakahānī (d. 731 H.)
- *Al-Tabyīn fī Sharḥ al-Arbaʿīn* by Imam Ibn Jamāh (d. 819 H.)

Al-Fat-ḥ al-Mubīn bi Sharḥ al-Arbacīn by Imam Ibn Ḥajar al-Haytamī (d. 973 H.)

Al-Mubīn al-Muīn li Fahm al-Arbacīn by Mullah ʿAlī al-Harawī al-Ḥanafī (d. 1014 H.)

- *Sharḥ al-Arbaʿīn al-Nawawiyyah* by Imam Sharnubī (d. 1348 H.)[4]

The Forty Hadiths of Imam al-Nawawī was first translated and annotated in Albanian by the esteemed and persecuted Hafiz Ibrahim Dalliu in 1934, titled *Hadíthi - Errbeàín.*[5]

In 1986, in Michigan, USA, Burhan Al-Din S. Fili published *Katërdhet Hadithe* (Forty Hadiths), emphasizing the duty and honor of striving towards virtue and success, foundations of gratification and spiritual well-being.[6]

---

[4] Ibn Hajar al-Askalani: *Sharh al-Arbain hadithan al-Nawawiyyah,* with notes from Riyad Isa Mansi and Abdulqadir Mustafa Taha, First published in Jordan, 2013, p. 44-46.

[5] Ibrahim Dalliu: *Me shënimet: Hadíthi – Errbeàín, Dyzet fjalë përmbledhse të Pejgamberit, alejhisselam të cilat i bâhen udhëheqse e plotsimit të çdo myslimani si kah besimi ashtû edhe kah moralet dhe kah veprat. Përmbledhë prej Imami Muhjiddini Neveviut.* Translated by Hafiz Ibrahim Dalliu. Given for free. Tiranë, Publishing House Shkodra, 1934.

[6] Burhan Al-Din S. Fili: *Katërdhet hadithe (Fjalë të profetit Muhammed A.S.) Zgjedhun prej: IMAM SHEREFED-DIN NEVEVIUT.* Translated and added notes by Burhan Al-Din S. Fili. First Published in 1986, Albanian Islamic Center Harper Wood, S, M I 48225.

Furthermore, Imam Ibn Rajab al-Hanbalī's work on the Forty Hadiths, translated by Albanian Islamic Scholar Mr. Nexhat Ibrahimi in Skopje in 1992 as *Dyzet Hadithe dhe Shtojca e Ibni Rexhepit* (Forty Hadith and the Subsidiary of Ibn Rajab), merits mention.[7]

Another significant work, *150 Hadithe* (150 Hadiths) by Imam Vehbi Ismaili, first published in Michigan in 1990 and later reprinted in 1993, forms part of his comprehensive writings compiled in eight volumes by Logos-A publishing house, Skopje, in 2009.[8]

In 2014, the Islamic Community Headquarters of Shkodër (Myftinia Shkodër) in Albania published a brochure titled *111 Hadithe të Përzgjedhura* (111 Selected Hadiths), providing Albanian readers with citations and insightful explanations.[9]

---

[7] In his epilogue, the esteemed translator shares this hopeful news: "As we now submit the anthology "*Forty Hadiths*" for publication, we have devoted ourselves fully to commenting on these hadiths. With Allah's help, we hope to complete this work successfully..." Nexhat Ibrahimi, Prizren, October 5, 1988.

[8] The author, Imam Vehbi Ismaili, makes an interesting note as he connects his work with the *Forty Hadiths* published in 1986. He writes, "In 1986, the Albanian Islamic Center of Michigan published the book *Forty Hadiths (Words of Prophet Muhammad)*, selected by Imam Sharafaddin Nawawi and annotated by Burhan El-Din S. Fili. This book was very well received by readers, and within a short time, all copies were sold out, prompting us to publish more copies. Since the publication of this book, our Center has received numerous requests to present a larger collection of Hadiths. In response to these requests, I began to select and translate one Hadith each day. When I reached 150 Hadiths, I decided to publish them." Imam Vehbi Ismaili, October 14, 1990, *Kolana e veprave të Imam Vehbi Ismaili*, Work 6, LOGOS-A, Skopje, 2009, pp. 11-12.

[9] "The 111 hadiths listed below are extracted from the first 1550 hadiths of the well-known book *Al-Jami' al-Saghir* by the distinguished scholar Imam Jalaluddin al-Suyuti (849-911 AH). *Al-Jami' al-Saghir*, contains an extensive collection of prophetic hadiths, which Imam al-Suyuti selected from his larger work *Jami' al-Jawami* where he compiled hadiths alphabetically." The explanations in the footnotes are sourced from the comprehensive book *Fayd al-Qadir* by the scholar Imam Muhammad Abdulrauf al-Munawi (924-1031 AH). In this work, Imam al-Munawi analyzed and explained all the hadiths in Imam Suyuti's book, also assessing the authenticity of each hadith. Selected, translated from Arabic, and adapted into Albanian by Muhammad B. Sytari, Shkodër, January 2014.

Today, Albanian readers have the opportunity to access a distinguished work on the Forty Hadiths, meticulously extracted from original sources, by the dedicated scholar and diligent researcher of beneficial knowledge, Imam Didmar Faja, Imam of the United Islamic Center of Arizona, USA. I read this marvelous book with great admiration, finding profound insights into love and reverence for the Prophet of Allah (peace be upon him) that deeply engage the reader.

I particularly value the author's incorporation of modern Islamic sources and the wisdom of classical scholars, enhancing the Albanian text. The author's use of relevant examples from contemporary realities enriches the commentary, drawing readers closer to Allah and His Messenger with conviction and obedience.

The author aptly cites esteemed scholars of earlier centuries such as Imam Taftazānī, Imam Qushayrī, and Imam Ghazālī, whose timeless wisdom and expertise in specific matters enrich the Albanian language rendition of this work.

I am confident that this new edition will benefit readers, especially Albanian Muslims in the diaspora, eager for such scholarly works. This book represents a significant step in qualitative writing by Imam Didmar Faja, transcending local confines to embrace a global horizon of knowledge and its benefits.

May Allah, the Merciful, accept this work as a testament of commitment and love for Him, the Almighty, and His mercy upon all the worlds, through the Prophet Muhammad (pbuh). Amin!

Imam Muhamed B. Sytari,
Mufti of Shkodër, Albania
Shkodër, 12 Rabiʿ al-Awwal 1436/January 3, 2015

Foreword by Sheikh Dr. Watheq Al-Obaidi, United States

Praise be to Allah, the Lord of all worlds, and may peace and blessings be upon the noblest of prophets and messengers, our master Muhammad, and upon his family and companions.

It is with great pride and deep appreciation that I extend my heartfelt thanks to His Eminence, Mufti and Imam Didmar Faja, whom we have come to know as a wise preacher who invites others to Allah with wisdom and good counsel. He is respected and cherished by scholars and people alike. Imam Faja has played a significant role in establishing Islamic centers in both the U.S. and Mexico. A devout scholar and Imam, he has a profound love for knowledge and scholars. I commend and congratulate his blessed efforts in explaining the book *Al-Arba'in Al-Nawawiyyah*, an invaluable text for preserving and teaching the Prophetic tradition (*sunnah*).

Imam Nawawi, may Allah have mercy on him, is one of the most distinguished scholars in Islamic history, contributing greatly to the fields of hadith and jurisprudence. His book *Al-Arba'in Al-Nawawiyyah* is among his most important works, containing 42 Prophetic hadiths that cover the foundations of faith, worship, and ethics.

I believe that the motivation behind Imam Nawawi's composition of this work is evident in his statement: "It has been narrated from Ali bin Abi Talib, Abdullah bin Masoud, Muadh bin Jabal, Ibn Umar, Ibn Abbas, Anas bin Malik, Abu Hurairah, and Abu Sa'id Al-Khudri, may Allah be pleased with them, through many chains of transmission and various narrations, that the Messenger of Allah, may peace and blessings be upon him, said: 'Whoever preserves for my community forty hadiths related to their religion, Allah will resurrect him on the Day of Judgment among the group of jurists and scholars.'"

Spreading the knowledge contained in *Al-Arba'in Al-Nawawiyyah* is of great significance, as it helps disseminate the Prophetic Sunnah and deepens Muslims' understanding of the fundamentals of their faith. It also serves as an essential resource for scholars and students of knowledge.

I pray that Allah accepts Imam Faja's efforts, and makes him among the inheritors of the prophets, who inherit both knowledge and wisdom, and that He makes us and him among the rightly guided scholars. May He also reward him abundantly and make him among the people of Paradise, and gather us all with the righteous scholars in the company of our beloved Prophet Muhammad, peace and blessings be upon him.

Finally, I offer my profound gratitude to Imam Faja for his blessed commentary, which will aid us in understanding the depths of the Prophetic Sunnah and in applying its teachings in our daily lives.

Sheikh Dr. Watheq Al-Obaidi,
President and Mufti of the Imam Abu Hanifa
Islamic Center in America,
Former Imam and Khateeb of
Imam Al-A'zam Mosque,
and Director of the Qadiriya
School in Baghdad

Introduction by the Author

All praise is due to Allah, the Creator and the All-Powerful. May His peace and blessings be upon all of His beloved Prophets and Messengers, especially His final and most beloved creation, our master and guide, Prophet Muhammad (peace be upon him). May His peace and blessings also be upon his pure family members, his honorable companions, and all those who follow his path.

Dear reader, I chose to comment on these hadiths not only because they are simple and concise, but also because they play a crucial role in shaping a truly balanced Muslim character. I originally wrote this book in 2014 in the Albanian language for an Albanian audience, due to the scarcity of literature on the commentary of Imam al-Nawawī's Forty Hadiths in Albanian. A year later, I began teaching at Madina Institute in Atlanta, USA, on the Principles of Islamic Jurisprudence according to the Ḥanafī school and the commentary of the Forty Hadiths of Imam al-Nawawī. Many students, friends, and community members requested that I translate the book into English to make the commentary more accessible. My motivation for this work was a profound desire to spread the teachings of our beloved Prophet (peace be upon him) while recognizing the countless blessings that come with doing so.

عَن أَبِي الدَّرداءِ، قال: قال رَسول الله صلى الله عليه وسلم: "مَن حَفِظَ عَلَى أُمَّتِي أَربَعِينَ حديثا مِن أَمرِ دِينِها، بَعَثَهُ اللَّهُ فَقِيهًا، وكُنتُ لَهُ يَومَ القِيامَةِ شافِعًا وشَهِيدًا".

Prophet Muhammad (peace be upon him) mentioned in a statement reported by his companion, Abū al-Dardā' (r.a.),

"Whoever memorizes and preserves forty hadiths relating to his religion, Allah will resurrect him on the Day of Judgment in the company of Islamic jurists and religious scholars, and I shall be an intercessor and a witness for him."[10]

Based on this hadith and many others transmitted through various chains of narration, many scholars have compiled forty hadiths, often providing commentary so people can learn and implement them. Among these scholars is Imam al-Nawawī from Nawā, Syria. His compilation became so renowned that it has been taught in mosques and traditional madrasas throughout the Islamic world. Perhaps God made Imam al-Nawawī's work so favorable and famous due to two factors: his devotion and sincerity in upholding the teachings of Prophet Muhammad (peace be upon him), and his scholarly expertise in carefully selecting hadiths that build and preserve a solid foundation of Islamic spirituality and practice in an individual.

Both classical and contemporary Muslim scholars have written commentaries on these forty hadiths. The first among them was Imam al-Nawawī himself. Many of the hadiths can be found in his commentary book, *Al-Minhāj fī sharḥ ṣaḥīḥ Muslim ibn al-Ḥajjāj*. Other notable commentators cited in this book include Imam al-Nawawī's student, ʿAlī ibn ʿAttār, who wrote *Sharḥ al-Arbaʿīn al-Nawawiyyah*, the famous theologian Imam Saʿd al-Dīn Masʿūd al-Taftāzānī, who authored *Sharḥ al-Taftāzānī ʿalā al-Aḥādīth al-Arbaʿīn al-Nawawiyyah*, and Imam ibn Rajab al-Hanbalī, known for *Jāmiʿ al-ʿUlūm wa al-Ḥikam.*

These commentaries, each with different styles and emphases, provide diverse insights into the hadiths. Through my humble efforts, I aimed to explain these hadiths in a way that addresses many present-day challenges, infused with the wisdom of classical scholars such as Imam Taftāzānī and Ibn Rajab. Many hadiths focus on morals and self-purification (*tazkiyah*),

---

[10] Abu Bakr Ahmed al-Bayhaqi: *Al-Jami' li Shu'ab al-Iman*, Maktabah al-Rushd, Riyadh, 2003, vol 3. p. 241 (the chain of transmission is weak).

offering solutions to current crises in morality and spirituality, supported by quotations from distinguished scholars like Imam Abū Hāmid Ghazālī, Shaykh Abū al-Qāsim al-Qushayrī, Shaykh ʿAbdul Qādir Jaylānī, Shaykh ʿAlī ibn ʿUthmān al-Hujwirī, and many others.

I suggest that readers not only read these hadiths once but revisit them often to reinforce their memory and practice. For families, a good time to read them might be after any prayer of the day or night, a few hadiths at a time. Imams can also read a few to their congregations after daily prayers.

In concluding this humble introduction, I pray to God to send His peace and blessings upon our beloved Prophet Muhammad (peace be upon him), his family members, his companions, Imam al-Nawawī, and all the scholars in the chains of narration (*asānīd*) of these hadiths, especially those who authorized us with *ijāzah* to narrate them through their chains back to our master, Prophet Muhammad (peace be upon him).

The one in need of God's Mercy and
His Forgiveness,
Didmar Faja
Glendale, Arizona,
1st Muharram 1440 (September 10th, 2018)

Transliteration and Notes

In this book, numerous essential Arabic words are utilized. For clarity and accessibility to English readers, I have employed standard transliterated letters, known as Arabic consonants. Below is a table presenting Arabic letters alongside their corresponding English equivalents.

English equivalent	Arabic letter	English equivalent	Arabic letter
A	ا	Ḍ	ض
B	ب	Ṭ	ط
T	ت	Z	ظ
Th	ث	ʿ [11]	ع
J	ج	Gh	غ
H	ح	F	ف
Kh	خ	Q	ق
D	د	K	ك
Dh	ذ	L	ل
R	ر	M	م
Z	ز	N	ن
S	س	W	و
Sh	ش	H	ه
Ṣ	ص	Y	ي

[11] ʿ represents the Arabic letter ع (ʿayn), which is a voiced pharyngeal fricative, a sound that doesn't have a direct equivalent in the Latin alphabet. The character " ʿ " is called a "turned comma" or "ayn" in transliteration systems.

Vowels and relevant marks

The circle symbolizes each letter of the Arabic language.

◌َ – The extended vowel A will be written as Ā or ā
◌ِ – The extended vowel I will be written as Ī or ī
◌ُ – The extended vowel U will be written as Ū
◌ً – Nunation "an"
◌ٍ – Nunation "in"
◌ٌ – Nunation "un"
◌ّ – Sign that doubles the letter or stresses on it.
◌ْ – Sign that indicates there is no following short vowel.

Abbreviations

The abbreviations used after the names of important figures in Islamic tradition serve specific purposes and carry particular meanings:

- (pbuh): This stands for "Peace Be Upon Him" and is used after mentioning Prophet Muhammad. It is a way for Muslims to show respect and invoke blessings upon him.
- (r.a.): This stands for "radiya Allahu anhu" (for a man), "radiya Allahu anha" (for a woman), or "radiya Allahu anhuma" (for two people, regardless of gender). It translates to "May Allah be pleased with him, her, or them," respectively. This phrase is used after the names of the companions of Prophet Muhammad to show respect and acknowledge their status.

Introduction to Hadith

From a linguistic perspective, "hadith" means an event or news. According to Muslim scholars, a hadith can be defined as a science that encompasses the words, deeds, reports, and qualities of the Messenger of Allah (pbuh). The first to narrate any hadith should be a companion of Prophet Muhammad (pbuh). According to some scholars, a hadith can also be accepted if the first narrator belongs to the generation immediately following the Prophet's companions (may God be pleased with them all), known as the *tābiʿīn*. Additionally, according to some, a hadith may be considered valid if narrated by a companion of the Prophet (pbuh) who did not hear it directly from the Prophet (pbuh) himself. Such a hadith is called "sent or transmitted" (*mursal*).

During the lifetime of Prophet Muhammad (pbuh), his companions were very attentive, not only in memorizing the Qur'an but also in memorizing the sayings of Prophet Muhammad (pbuh). They conveyed those sayings to their next generations, who in turn conveyed them to the following generation, continuing in a chain until the present day. Prophet Muhammad (pbuh) encouraged the study, memorization, and narration of hadith. He stated in a hadith narrated by ʿAbdullāh ibn ʿAmr,

"بَلِّغُوا عَنِّي وَلَوْ آيَةً وَحَدِّثُوا عَنْ بَنِي إِسْرَائِيلَ وَلا حَرَج، وَمَنْ كَذَبَ عَلَيَّ مُتَعَمِّدًا فَلْيَتَبَوَّأْ مَقْعَدَهُ مِنَ النَّارِ".

"Convey from me even an Ayah of the Qur'an; relate traditions from Jewish people, and there is no restriction on that; but he who deliberately forges a lie against me let him have his abode in Hell."[12]

For those who narrate and teach hadiths to the others, the Messenger of Allah (pbuh) has supplicated,

"اللَّهُمَّ ارْحَمْ خُلَفَاءَنَا"، قُلْنَا: يَا رَسُولَ اللَّهِ، وَمَا خُلَفَاؤُكُمْ؟ قَالَ: "الَّذِينَ يَأْتُونَ مِنْ بَعْدِي، يَرْوُونَ أَحَادِيثِي وَسُنَّتِي، وَيُعَلِّمُونَهَا النَّاسَ".

"O God! Have mercy on our successors!" We said, "O Messenger of Allah! Who are your successors?" He said, "Those who will come after me, conveying my sayings and my tradition, and teaching them to the people."[13]

Studying hadith can provide an accurate understanding of the Qur'an. Many verses are explained by Prophet Muhammad (pbuh) himself and narrated to us through hadiths. Additionally, there are hadiths that explain the reasons behind the revelations (*asbāb al-nuzūl*) of particular surahs or verses of the Qur'an.

The prophetic tradition (*sunnah*) of Prophet Muhammad (pbuh) is the second main source in Islam after the Qur'an. According to the Qur'an, Muslims are therefore required to follow his example. As stated in the Qur'an,

"لَقَدْ كَانَ لَكُمْ فِي رَسُولِ اللَّهِ أُسْوَةٌ حَسَنَةٌ لِّمَن كَانَ يَرْجُو اللَّهَ وَالْيَوْمَ الْآخِرَ وَذَكَرَ اللَّهَ كَثِيرًا"

---

[12] Ahmad Ibn Hanbal: *Musnad Ahmad ibn Hanbal*, Dar al-Hadith, Cairo, 1995, vol. 6, p. 42.

[13] Sulayman ibn Ahmad al-Tabarani, *Al-Mu'jam al-Awsat*, Dar al-Haramayn, Cairo, 1995, vol. 6, p. 77.

"There has certainly been for you in the Messenger of Allah an excellent pattern for anyone whose hope is in Allah and the Last Day and (who) remembers Allah often."[14]

Implementing the above-mentioned verse from the Qur'an requires one to hear, read, and possibly memorize various hadiths. Unlike the Qur'an, some hadiths may be considered weak due to transmission defects, while others may be identified as fabricated. For this reason, hadith scholars engaged in a rigorous evaluation of hadiths and categorized them into four distinct categories:

1. Authentic Hadith (*ḥadīth ṣaḥīḥ*)
2. Good or sound Hadith (*ḥadīth ḥasan*)
3. Weak Hadith (*ḥadīth ḍaʿīf*)
4. Fabricated Hadith (*ḥadīth mawḍūʿ*)

When it comes to determining the ruling of an Islamic religious practice, scholars base their rulings on authentic (*ṣaḥīḥ*) hadiths and some consider the good (*ḥasan*) hadiths. Generally, they have advised using weak (*ḍaʿīf*) hadiths for understanding the virtues of righteous deeds, reminders, and similar purposes. As for fabricated hadiths, scholars have compiled books listing them and have instructed people not to use or refer to them. This caution is due to a statement from the Messenger of Allah (pbuh), narrated by his cousin and companion Ali (r.a.), which emphasizes the importance of avoiding falsehood in attributing statements to the Prophet:

"لَا تَكْذِبُوا عَلَيَّ، فَإِنَّهُ مَنْ كَذَبَ عَلَيَّ فَلْيَلِجْ النَّارَ".

[14] Qur'an (33:21). Saheeh International will be used as the reference for the English translation of the Qur'an throughout this book. The specific edition referenced is: Saheeh International. *The Qur'an: English Meanings and Notes*. Jeddah: Al-Muntada Al-Islam Trust, 2011.

"Do not invent lies about me, for whoever invents lies about me will enter Hell."[15]

The companions of Prophet Muhammad (pbuh) mainly taught and preserved hadith orally. Later, recognizing the increasing importance of preserving it in writing, future generations compiled many books of hadith. This way, hadith could be better preserved, and upcoming generations could access it more readily.

During the third generation, that of the tābiʿ al-tābiʿīn, Imam Muḥammad Shaybānī compiled a book of transmitted hadiths from the eponymous founder of the first Islamic school of jurisprudence, Imam Abū Ḥanīfah (d. 148/767). This noteworthy book is known as Kitāb al-Āthār. Imam Shaybānī also compiled another significant book of transmitted hadiths called Muwaṭṭa', attributed to Imam Mālik ibn Anas (d. 179/795), the founder of the second Islamic school of jurisprudence. Imam Muḥammad ibn Idrīs al-Shāfiʿī (d. 204/820), the founder of the third Islamic school of jurisprudence, transmitted different hadiths in his famous book, Musnad al-Imām al-Shāfiʿī. Not long after, another voluminous book of hadith called Musnad Imām Aḥmad was compiled by the founder of the fourth Islamic school of jurisprudence, Imam Aḥmad ibn Ḥanbal (241/855).

After this phase, various scholars wrote books of their narrated hadiths, and six among them stood out because of their level of accuracy:

- *Ṣaḥīḥ al-Bukhārī*, written by Imam Muḥammad bin Ismāʿīl al-Bukhārī (d. 256/870).
- *Ṣaḥīḥ Muslim*, written by Imam Muslim ibn al-Ḥajjāj (d. 261/875).

Jāmic al-Tirmīdhī, written by Imam Muḥammad ibn cĪsā al-Tirmidhī (d. 279/892).

Sunan Abī Dāvūd, written by Imam Abū Dāvūd Sulaymān ibn al-Ashcath al-Azdī al-Sijistānī (d. 275/889).

Sunan al-Nasāī, written by Imam Aḥmad ibn Shucayb al-Nasāī (d. 303/915).

---

[15] Shamsuddin al-Kirmani: *Al-Kawakib al-Darari fī Sharh Sahih al-Bukhari*, Dar Ihya al-Turath al-Arabi, Beirut, 2nd edition, 1981, vol. 2, p. 109-11.

Sunan ibn Mājah, written by Imam Muḥammad ibn Jazīd ibn Mājah al-Rabcī al-Qazwīnī (d. 273/887).

Ṣaḥīḥ al-Bukhārī and *Ṣaḥīḥ Muslim* are considered by the majority of hadith scholars to contain only authentic hadiths, while the other four collections have a small number of weak hadiths.

The Life of Imam al-Nawawī

His name was Muḥy al-Dīn Abū Zakariyyā Yaḥyā ibn Sharaf al-Ḥizāmī al-Nawawī.[16] He was born in the middle of the Islamic month of Muḥarram 631 AH, which corresponds to 1233 according to the Gregorian calendar. He was born in Nawā, south of Damascus, Syria, and came from a modest family.[17] When al-Nawawī was young, his father noticed that his son had an exceptional devotion to the Qur'an, so he decided to take him to Damascus, which at that time had over three hundred institutes teaching Islamic sciences.

His teachers and students

Imam al-Nawawī had more than twenty distinguished teachers: Abū Ibrahīm Is-ḥāq el-Maghribī, Abū Muḥammad ʿAbd al-Raḥmān al-Maqdisī, Abū Ḥafṣ cUmar al-Rabacī, Abū al-Ḥasan al-Arbīlī, Abū Al-Fat-ḥ ʿUmar bin Bundār al-Shāficī, Fakhr al-Dīn al-Mālikī, Muḥammad bin ʿAbdullāh al-Xhiyyānī, Abū Is-ḥāq Ibrāhīm bin cĪsā al-Murādī al-Andalūsī, Abū al-Beqā Khālid binYūsuf al-Nābulsī, ʿAbd al-Raḥmān bin Muḥammad bin Aḥmad al-Maqdisī, Ḍiyā al-Ḥanafī, Muḥammad bin

[16] The word "Abu" means father. Although Imam al-Nawawī had no children and was never married, "Abu Zakariyyā" is used as a nickname or typical epithet among Arabs.

[17] Ala al-Din Ali ibn al-Attar: *Tuhfat al-Talibin fi Tarjumat al-Imam al-Nawawi*, Dar al-Athariyyah, Amman, 2007, p. 43.

Muḥammad al-Bakrī, Abū al-Faḍāil ʿAbd al-Karīm bin ʿAbd al-Ṣamad, Ibrahīm bin ʿAlī al-Wāsiṭī, etc.[18]

Imam al-Nawawī had many students. The following are some of his distinguished ones: ʿAlā al-dīn bin ʿAṭṭār, Ibn ʿAbbās Aḥmad bin Ibrāhīm, ʿAbd al-ʿAbbās al-Jaʿfarī, ʿAbd al-ʿAbbās Aḥmad bin Faraḥ, Rashīd Ismācil bin Mucallim al-Ḥanafī, Abū ʿAbdullāh al-Ḥanbalī, Abū al-ʿAbbās Al-Vāsiṭī, etc.

About his virtues

Ibn ʿĀṭṭār, the student of Imam al-Nawawī, in his book *Tuḥfat al-Ṭālibīn*, mentioned that Imam Ikhmajmī stated the following in regard to the great virtues of Imam al-Nawawī: "Shaykh Muḥy al-Dīn was a follower of the path of the Prophet's companions. I have no knowledge of anyone who follows their path as he does."[19]

Imam al-Nawawī was an example of those scholars who acquired knowledge not as a means to boast but to get closer to God and serve His creation. His father mentioned that al-Nawawī was someone who followed his teachers closely. He was very attentive in worshipful acts of prayer, fasting, and other righteous ones. He would always stay away from forbidden deeds and would not waste his time. After the passing away of his teacher, Shaykh Abū Ibrahīm Is-ḥāq, Imam al-Nawawī became even more zealous in his knowledge and his righteous deeds.[20]

He was always busy with knowledge, to such a level where even when walking in the streets he would busy himself with the repetition of what he already knew. In regard to his remarkable values, the well-known judge of that time, Muḥammad bin cAbd al-Qīr al-Anṣārī, mentioned to Ibn ʿĀṭṭār, "If the author of the *Al-Risālah*,[21] Imam al-Qushayrī, would

---

[18] Ibid. p. 42.

[19] Ibid. p. 69.

[20] Ibid. p. 48.

[21] A famous book known for its scholarly competence on issues related to the refinement of the soul, levels of devotion to God, fear, and obedience to Him. It contains prominent passages from the lives of many distinguished mystics of the time.

have known your teacher and his teacher, he would not have mentioned anyone before them because they intertwined perfectly well between knowledge, achievement, devotion, distancing from forbidden things, mature statements, and many more traits."[22]

Demonstrated miracles (*karāmāt*)

Often, God the Almighty endows some of his righteous servants with the ability to perform miracles. This is to indicate His existence and also to demonstrate the esteemed position that some of His close servants (*awliyā' Allāh*) have with Him. The miracles that God performs through His chosen servants are not attainable by studying thoroughly the science of physics, nor through technological development. Among those who God graced with the ability of miracles was also Imam al-Nawawī. The following are some instances where different individuals have testified to those miracles.

Imam Shams al-Dīn al-Sakhawī, in his biography book of Imam al-Nawawī, *Al-Manhal al-'Adhb fi Tarjamat Quṭb al-Awliyā'*, narrates the following story from the father of Imam al-Nawawī:

> One night, my seven-year-old son was sleeping near me. It was the twenty-seventh night of Ramadan. Then he woke up in the middle of the night and after waking me up as well, he said to me; "Oh, father! What is this light that has filled our home?" He woke up all the people in the house but none of us saw anything. I realized that it was the Night of Decree (*Laylat al-Qadr*).[23]

The scholar Abū al-Ḥasan of Damascus, who lived during the time of Imam Nawawī, also narrates,

> I had an illness in my leg. Imam Nawawī came and sat near me. Then, he

[22] Ala al-Din Ali ibn al-Attar: *Tuhfat al-Talibin fi Tarjumat al-Imam al-Nawawi*, p. 49.

[23] Shams al-Din Muhammad al-Sakhawi: *Al-Manhal al-Adhb fi Tarxhamet Qutb al-Awliya' al-Nawawi*, Dar al-Kutub al-Ilmiyyah, Beirut, 2005, p. 11.

> started to talk about patience. Every word that he spoke was soothing, gradually removing the pain little by little, until all the pain was gone. I realized that this happened because of the blessings bestowed upon him.[24]

On another occasion, the Imam himself mentioned,

> Once, I was sick in the Islamic school (madrasah) of al-Ravāḥiyyat. My father, my brothers, and some relatives were sleeping beside me. Meanwhile, God relieved my sickness and since I had missed some invocations, I began mentioning Allah (dhikr) and glorifying Him. I performed this dhikr silently and loudly.
> Suddenly, I saw an old, yet good-looking man. He was performing ablution in the middle of the night, right at the fountain (where one makes ablution). After he performed the ablution, he approached me and said, "O my child! Do not mention Allah because you bother your father, your brothers, relatives, and everyone who is in this *madrasah*."
> I told him, "O elder! Who are you?"
> He replied, "Let me be who I used to be."
> I understood that this was Satan himself (*Iblīs*) and I said, "I seek refuge with Allah from Satan, the accursed." I raised my voice glorifying Allah, while he left and approached the door of the school. My father and the people there heard my voice. As I came to the door, to my surprise, the door was locked. I looked around, but I did not find anyone, except those who were there earlier.
> Then my father said, "O Abū Zakariyyā! What happened?" I told him what had happened. They were all surprised and then we started to pray and thank Allah."[25]

---

[24] Ibid. p. 41.

[25] Ala al-Din Ali ibn al-Attar: *Tuhfat al-Talibin fi Tarjumat al-Imam al-Nawawi*, p. 52.

Some of his works

Imam al-Nawawī had profound knowledge in different Islamic disciplines, especially in hadith, Islamic Jurisprudence (*fiqh*), Qur'an, Arabic, and Sufism. He wrote many books and they became fundamental teachings of each respective discipline. Here are some of his works:

- *Rawḍāt al-Ṭālibīn* – A book written on Islamic Jurisprudence according to the Shāfi'ī school.
- *Al-Majmū' Sharḥ al-Muhadh-dhib* – A commentary book on the Pillars of Islam according to the Islamic juristic rules of the Shāfi'ī school.
- *Al-Minhāj fi Sharḥ Ṣaḥīḥ Muslim ibn al-Ḥajjāj* – A commentary book on the authentic hadith compilation of Imam Muslim.
- *Riyāḍ al-Ṣāliḥīn min Kalām Sayyid al-Mursalīn* – A famous compilation book of hadiths.
- *Al-Adhkār* – A book of supplications based on the sayings of Prophet Muhammad (pbuh).
- *Bustān al-'Ārifīn* – A book on devotion and Sufism. Imam al-Nawawī passed away before completing this book.
- *Al-Arba'īn* – The book on forty hadiths.
- *Al-Tibyān fi Ādāb Ḥimla al-Qur'ān* – A book on the importance and manners of reading the Qur'an.

His death

Ibn 'Aṭṭār mentioned that approximately two months before his death, a poor person came to Imam al-Nawawī and offered him a teakettle:

Imam accepted the gift. This was something strange because he never had accepted gifts. Imam told me that he accepted two gifts he could not refuse: the teakettle and the shoes, which he would use for his trip. Then, another man came and told him the time for the trip had come. Before his trip, he gathered his students and visited the graves of his teachers, read Qur'an, cried, and prayed for them. Then he visited his beloved ones.[26]

---

26 Ala al-Din Ali ibn al-Attar: *Tuhfat al-Talibin fi Tarjumat al-Imam al-Nawawi*, p. 96-8.

Ibn Aṭṭār mentioned that during this time he had seen in him things that would require writing voluminous books to describe.

Later, Imam traveled to Quds[27] and Khalīl.[28] After the visit to the Holy Land, he returned to his birthplace, Nawā. Meanwhile, he got sick at his father's home. I went to him immediately. When he saw me, he was very delighted and later told me to get back to my family. After four days, the announcement of his passing away was made in the mosque of Damascus. He passed away when he was 44 years old, in the year 676 AH (corresponding to 1278 AD).[29]

---

[27] Palestine, where the Al-Aqsa Mosque is located. This mosque is one of the three holy mosques in Islam. A prayer there is equivalent to the reward of 500 prayers in other places, except for the Masjid al-Haram in Mecca and the Prophet's Mosque in Medina.

[28] City in Palestine where the prophets of God, such as Ibrahim, Is-haq, Ya'qub, Yusuf, etc., are buried.

[29] Ala al-Din Ali ibn al-Attar: *Tuhfat al-Talibin fi Tarjumat al-Imam al-Nawawi*, p. 96-8.

Imam al-Nawawī's Preface[30]

In the Name of Allah, Most Merciful and Compassionate

Praise be to God, Lord of the Worlds, the Sustainer of the heavens and earth, the Disposer of all created beings, the Sender of Messengers, may God's blessing and peace be upon them, to those who are legally responsible, so as to guide them and elucidate (to them) the ordinances of the religion with conclusive proofs and clear evidences. I praise Him for all His blessings and ask Him for more of His favor and generosity.

I also bear witness that there is no deity but God, the One, the All-Compelling, the Generous and the Oft-Forgiving. And I bear witness that Muhammad is His servant and messenger, beloved and intimate friend, the best of all created beings, who was honored with the noble Qur'an—the continuous miracle throughout the years—and with clear ways for those seeking guidance; and who was further singled out to have the most comprehensive speech and tolerance of religion. And may God's blessings and peace be upon him and upon all the prophets, their households and upon all the righteous among people.

To proceed: we have narrated from ʿAlī ibn Abī Ṭālib, ʿAbdullāh ibn Masʿūd, Muʿādh ibn Jabal, Abū al-Dardā', Ibn ʿUmar, Ibn ʿAbbās, Anas ibn Mālik, Abū Hurayrah and Abū Saʿīd al-Khudrī, may God be pleased with them, from many chains of transmission and in variegated versions that God's Messenger, may God's blessings and peace be upon him, said,

---

[30] This is the translation of his original preface from *Al-Arbaʿīn*.

"Whosoever preserves for my Community forty hadiths relating to matters of its religion, God will resurrect him on Judgement Day with the scholars of Sacred Law and the scholars of sacred knowledge," and, in another version, "God will resurrect him as a scholar of Sacred Law and sacred knowledge." The version of Abū al-Dardā' has "and I shall be a witness and intercessor for him on Judgement Day"; and, in the version of Ibn Mas'ūd, "he shall be told: enter from any of the gates of Paradise you wish to enter"; and, in the version of Ibn 'Umar, "he shall be recorded amongst the group of scholars of sacred knowledge and assembled amongst the martyrs." Hadith masters agree that this hadith is weak even though its chains of transmission are diverse.

Scholars, may God be pleased with them, have authored countless books in this field. The first in this field is 'Abdullāh ibn al-Mubārak, then Muḥammad ibn Aslam al-Ṭūsī, the pious scholar, then al-Ḥasan ibn Sufyān al-Nasawī, Abū Bakr al-Ājūri, Abū Bakr Muḥammad ibn Ibrahīm al-Aṣfahānī, al-Dāraquṭnī, al-Ḥākim, Abū Nu'aym [al-Aṣfahānī], Abū 'Abd al-Raḥmān al-Sulamī, Abū Sa'īd al-Mālīmī, Abū 'Uthmān al-Bābūnī, 'Abdullāh ibn Muḥammad al-Anṣārī, Abū Bakr al-Bayhaqī, and countless other people from the first and later generations of Muslims. Hence, I have sought God's guidance to gather forty prophetic sayings in emulation of these eminent masters and preservers of Islam.

The scholars of sacred knowledge agree about the permissibility of using weak prophetic traditions as evidence for performing works of virtue. Nonetheless, my reliance is not on this above-mentioned tradition. I am rather relying on his saying, may God's blessings and peace be upon him, in rigorously-authenticated hadiths, "Let those present among you inform those who are absent," and on his saying, may God's blessings and peace be upon him, "God bestows beauty and light on the person who hears my speech, remembers it and then passes it on as he has heard it."

Furthermore, there are among the scholars of sacred knowledge those who have gathered forty hadiths relating to tenets of faith, while others chose particular questions of Sacred Law, or jihad, or non-attachment (to the world), or good conduct, or the sermons of the Prophet, may God's blessings and peace be upon him—all of which are noble aims, may God be pleased with those who sought to compile them.

I have decided to compile forty hadiths that are more important than all these aims, and which further comprise all of them. Each hadith is a great rule of the religion, described by scholars of sacred knowledge as an axis of Islam, or that it is half of Islam or its third, or something similar. In these forty hadiths, I confine myself to those rigorously authenticated, most of which are in the rigorously-authenticated collections of al-Bukhārī and Muslim. I shall mention them without their chains of transmission so as to facilitate their memorization and widen their benefit, God willing, and then I shall follow them by a chapter in which I explain difficult words.

Anyone desiring the Afterlife ought to know these hadiths in view of what they contain of important matters and of reminders of all acts of obedience; this is obvious to anyone who has bothered to think. My reliance is on God, I seek refuge in Him and to Him I consign my affairs. Praise and blessing are His, and through Him is success and protection from sin.

HADITH 1

الحديث الأول

Actions Are Judged by Intentions

عَنْ أَمِيرِ الْمُؤْمِنِينَ أَبِي حَفْصٍ عُمَرَ بْنِ الْخَطَّابِ رَضِيَ اللهُ عَنْهُ قَالَ: سَمِعْتُ رَسُولَ اللَّهِ صلى الله عليه وسلم يَقُولُ:

"إِنَّمَا الْأَعْمَالُ بِالنِّيَّاتِ، وَإِنَّمَا لِكُلِّ امْرِئٍ مَا نَوَى، فَمَنْ كَانَتْ هِجْرَتُهُ إِلَى اللَّهِ وَرَسُولِهِ فَهِجْرَتُهُ إِلَى اللَّهِ وَرَسُولِهِ، وَمَنْ كَانَتْ هِجْرَتُهُ لِدُنْيَا يُصِيبُهَا أَوْ امْرَأَةٍ يَنْكِحُهَا فَهِجْرَتُهُ إِلَى مَا هَاجَرَ إِلَيْهِ".

رَوَاهُ إِمَامَا الْمُحَدِّثِينَ أَبُو عَبْدِ اللهِ مُحَمَّدُ بنُ إِسْمَاعِيل بن إِبْرَاهِيم بن الْمُغِيرَة بن بَرْدِزبَه الْبُخَارِيُّ الْجُعْفِيُّ، وَأَبُو الْحُسَيْنِ مُسْلِمُ بنُ الْحَجَّاج بن مُسْلِم الْقُشَيْرِيُّ النَّيْسَابُورِيُّ رَضِيَ اللهُ عَنْهُمَا فِي "صَحِيحَيْهِمَا" اللذَينِ هُمَا أَصَحُّ الْكُتُبِ الْمُصَنَّفَةِ.

The leader of the believers Abū Ḥafs ʿUmar bin al-Khaṭṭāb (may God be pleased with him) said: I heard the Messenger of Allah (pbuh) say,

"Actions are (judged) by intentions; therefore, each man will have what he intended. As for he whose migration was to Allah and His Messenger, then his migration is indeed to Allah and His Messenger; but he whose migration was for some worldly gain, or for a wife he might marry, then his migration is to that for which he migrated."

Related by the two Imams of hadith scholars, Abū ʿAbdillāh Muḥammad bin Ismāʿīl bin Ibrāhīm bin al-Mughīrah bin Bardizbah al-Bukhārī al-Juʿfī and Abū al-Ḥusayn Muslim bin al-Ḥajjāj bin Muslim al-Qushayrī al-Naysābūrī, may God be pleased with them both. They both report this hadith in their sound compilations, which are the most authentic compiled hadith books.

Themes

- The significance of intention: Understanding the profound importance of intention (*niyyah*) in Islamic practice and how it shapes the validity and reward of deeds.
- Distinguishing between migration for the sake of God and other reasons: Exploring the concept of migration in Islam, particularly the spiritual and religious significance of migrating solely for the sake of pleasing Allah versus other motivations.

Explanation

Many scholars who compiled collections of hadiths have placed this hadith at the forefront of their works. This is intended to emphasize to readers or students of hadith that before embarking on any action, they must purify their intentions. Indeed, many scholars have considered this hadith to encapsulate a third of Islam.

Intention resides within the heart, and its importance often surpasses the deed itself or its outcomes. In Islam, the spiritual state of the heart and the inner intentions hold a profound significance, capable of drawing one closer to experiencing the presence of God beyond the physical actions of the body. Thus, because intention originates from within the human soul, it can attract Allah's blessings and rewards, even if circumstances prevent the intended action from being carried out. Prophet Muhammad (pbuh) underscored the primacy of the inner self over the outer self in the following hadith:

عَنْ ابْنِ عَبَّاسٍ رَضِيَ اللَّهُ عَنْهُمَا، عَنْ النَّبِيِّ صَلَّى اللَّهُ عَلَيْهِ وَسَلَّمَ، فِيمَا يَرْوِي عَنْ رَبِّهِ عَزَّ وَجَلَّ، قَالَ: "إِنَّ اللَّهَ كَتَبَ الْحَسَنَاتِ وَالسَّيِّئَاتِ، ثُمَّ بَيَّنَ ذَلِكَ: فَمَنْ هَمَّ بِحَسَنَةٍ فَلَمْ يَعْمَلْهَا، كَتَبَهَا اللَّهُ لَهُ عِنْدَهُ حَسَنَةً كَامِلَةً، فَإِنْ هُوَ هَمَّ بِهَا فَعَمِلَهَا، كَتَبَهَا اللَّهُ لَهُ عِنْدَهُ عَشْرَ حَسَنَاتٍ، إِلَى سَبْعِمِائَةِ ضِعْفٍ، إِلَى أَضْعَافٍ كَثِيرَةٍ، وَمَنْ هَمَّ بِسَيِّئَةٍ فَلَمْ يَعْمَلْهَا، كَتَبَهَا اللَّهُ لَهُ عِنْدَهُ حَسَنَةً كَامِلَةً، فَإِنْ هُوَ هَمَّ بِهَا فَعَمِلَهَا، كَتَبَهَا اللَّهُ سَيِّئَةً وَاحِدَةً". رَوَاهُ الْبُخَارِيُّ وَمُسْلِمُ

The son of ʿAbbās (may Allah be pleased with them both) narrated from the Messenger of Allah (pbuh) who related from his Lord (glorified and exalted be He) that He said,

"Allah has written down the good deeds and the bad ones. Then He explained it (by saying that) he who has intended a good deed and has not done it, Allah writes it down with Himself as a full good deed, but if he has intended it and has done it, Allah writes it down with Himself as from ten good deeds to seven hundred times, or many times over. But if he has intended a bad deed and has not done it, Allah writes it down with Himself as a full good deed, but if he has intended it and has done it, Allah writes it down as one bad deed."

Related by al-Bukhāri and Muslim.[31]

Although spirituality transcends formalities, when intertwined, they can bring tranquility (*sakīnah*) to someone's heart. Regarding migration (*hijrah*) for the sake of God and His Messenger, in the latter part of the hadith, the Prophet (pbuh) did not specify a reward for such an action; instead, he stated, "...then his migration is indeed to Allah and His Messenger." This statement echoes a hadith Qudsi reported by Abū Hurayrah,

عن أبي هريرة رضي الله عنه، قال: قال رسول الله صلى الله عليه وسلم: قَالَ اللَّهُ عَزَّ وَجَلَّ: "كُلُّ عَمَلِ ابْنِ آدَمَ لَهُ إلا الصِّيَامَ فَإِنَّهُ لِي وَأَنَا أَجْزِي بِهِ".

[31] Abu Bakr Ahmed al-Bayhaqi: *Al-Jami' li Shu'ab al-Iman*, vol 1. p. 514.

The Messenger of Allah (pbuh) said, "Allah the Exalted and Majestic said: 'Every act of the son of Adam is for him, except the fasting which is for Me, and I will reward him for it.'"[32]

Generous people, when they intend to give a profound gift, often keep it concealed as a surprise until the right moment arrives to reveal it. This unexpected gesture brings great joy to the recipient. Similarly, the reward of fasting or migrating for the sake of Allah is kept as a surprise for the believer.

The hadith also addresses migration for other reasons, such as material gain or marriage proposals. In these cases, Prophet Muhammad (pbuh) does not forbid such migrations but indicates that the reward will be based on the intentions behind them.

While discussing migration in this hadith, it's important to consider both physical and spiritual dimensions. The physical aspect is clearly explained in the hadith. Regarding the spiritual aspect, it involves migrating from what Islam prohibits to what it commands or permits. Prophet Muhammad (pbuh) mentioned in a hadith narrated by Abdullāh Ibn 'Amr,

"أَلْمُسْلِمُ مَنْ سَلِمَ الْمُسْلِمُونَ مِنْ لِسَانِهِ وَيَدِهِ، وَالْمُهَاجِرُ مَنْ هَجَرَ مَا نَهَى اللَّهُ عَنْهُ".

"A Muslim is the one who avoids harming Muslims with his tongue or his hands. And an emigrant (*muhājir*) is the one who gives up (abandons) all what Allah has forbidden."[33]

For those engaged in deeper spiritual practices, *hijrah* can also signify a spiritual journey where one detaches their heart from the transient and attaches it to the Eternal Creator.

---

[32] Abu Abdurrahman Al-Nasai: *Musnad al-Nasai al-Mujtaba*, Dar al-Risalah al-Alamiyyah, Riyadh, 2018, v. 4, p. 256.

[33] Shamsuddin al-Kirmani: *Al-Kawakib al-Darari fi Sharh Sahih al-Bukhari*, vol. 1, p. 89.

HADITH 2

الحديث الثاني

The Hadith of Gabriel

عَنْ عُمَرَ رَضِيَ اللهُ عَنْهُ أَيْضًا قَالَ: "بَيْنَمَا نَحْنُ جُلُوسٌ عِنْدَ رَسُولِ اللَّهِ صلى الله عليه وسلم ذَاتَ يَوْمٍ، إذْ طَلَعَ عَلَيْنَا رَجُلٌ شَدِيدُ بَيَاضِ الثِّيَابِ، شَدِيدُ سَوَادِ الشَّعْرِ، لَا يُرَى عَلَيْهِ أَثَرُ السَّفَرِ، وَلَا يَعْرِفُهُ مِنَّا أَحَدٌ. حَتَّى جَلَسَ إلَى النَّبِيِّ صلى الله عليه وسلم. فَأَسْنَدَ رُكْبَتَيْهِ إلَى رُكْبَتَيْهِ، وَوَضَعَ كَفَّيْهِ عَلَى فَخِذَيْهِ، وَقَالَ: يَا مُحَمَّدُ أَخْبِرْنِي عَنْ الْإِسْلَامِ فَقَالَ رَسُولُ اللَّهِ صلى الله عليه وسلم الْإِسْلَامُ أَنْ تَشْهَدَ أَنْ لَا إلَهَ إلَّا اللَّهُ وَأَنَّ مُحَمَّدًا رَسُولُ اللَّهِ، وَتُقِيمَ الصَّلَاةَ، وَتُؤْتِيَ الزَّكَاةَ، وَتَصُومَ رَمَضَانَ، وَتَحُجَّ الْبَيْتَ إنْ اسْتَطَعْت إلَيْهِ سَبِيلًا قَالَ: صَدَقْت. فَعَجِبْنَا لَهُ يَسْأَلُهُ وَيُصَدِّقُهُ قَالَ: فَأَخْبِرْنِي عَنْ الْإِيمَانِ قَالَ: أَنْ تُؤْمِنَ بِاَللَّهِ وَمَلَائِكَتِهِ وَكُتُبِهِ وَرُسُلِهِ وَالْيَوْمِ الْآخِرِ، وَتُؤْمِنَ بِالْقَدَرِ خَيْرِهِ وَشَرِّهِ قَالَ: صَدَقْت. قَالَ: فَأَخْبِرْنِي عَنْ الْإِحْسَانِ قَالَ: أَنْ تَعْبُدَ اللَّهَ كَأَنَّك تَرَاهُ، فَإِنْ لَمْ تَكُنْ تَرَاهُ فَإِنَّهُ يَرَاك قَالَ: فَأَخْبِرْنِي عَنْ السَّاعَةِ. قَالَ: مَا الْمَسْئُولُ عَنْهَا بِأَعْلَمَ مِنْ السَّائِلِ قَالَ: فَأَخْبِرْنِي عَنْ أَمَارَاتِهَا؟ قَالَ: أَنْ تَلِدَ الْأَمَةُ رَبَّتَهَا، وَأَنْ تَرَى الْحُفَاةَ الْعُرَاةَ الْعَالَةَ رِعَاءَ الشَّاءِ يَتَطَاوَلُونَ فِي الْبُنْيَانِ. ثُمَّ انْطَلَقَ، فَلَبِثْتُ مَلِيًّا، ثُمَّ قَالَ: يَا عُمَرُ أَتَدْرِي مَنْ السَّائِلُ؟ قُلْتُ: اللَّهُ وَرَسُولُهُ أَعْلَمُ. قَالَ: فَإِنَّهُ جِبْرِيلُ أَتَاكُمْ يُعَلِّمُكُمْ دِينَكُمْ".

رَوَاهُ مُسْلِمٌ.

It is also reported from ʿUmar (r.a.) that he said: While we were one day sitting with the Messenger of Allah (pbub) there appeared before us a man dressed in very white clothes and had very black hair. No traces of traveling were noticeable on him, and none of us knew him.

He sat down close by the Prophet (pbuh), rested his knees against the knees of the Prophet (pbuh) and placed his palms over his thighs and said, "O Muhammad! Inform me about Islam."

The Messenger of Allah (pbuh) mentioned: "Islam is that you should declare that there is no God other than Allah and that Muhammad (pbuh) is the Messenger of Allah, that you should establish the Prayer (*ṣalat*), give out charity (*zakāt*), fast during Ramadan, and perform the Pilgrimage (*ḥajj*) to the House (the Kaaba) if you have the ability (or the means) to do so."

He said, "You have spoken the truth." We were surprised, for he questioned and affirmed him. Then he said, "Inform me about faith (*īmān*)."

He (the Prophet) answered, "It is that you believe in Allah and His angels and His Books and His Messengers and in the Last Day, and in destiny (*qadar*), both in its good and in its evil aspects."

He said, "You have spoken the truth." Then he (the man) said, "Inform me about achieving excellence when performing deeds (*iḥsān*)."

He (the Prophet) answered, "It is that you should worship (or serve) Allah as you could see Him, even though you cannot see Him, yet, He sees you."

He said, "Inform me about the Hour."

He (the Prophet) said, "About that, the one questioned knows no more than the questioner."

So, he said, "Well, inform me about its signs."

He said, "They are that the slave-girl will give birth to her mistress and that you will see the barefooted ones, the naked, the destitute, the herdsmen of the sheep (competing with each other) in raising high buildings."

Later, (the man) went away. I waited a while, and then he (the Prophet) said, "O 'Umar, do you know who the questioner was?" I said, "Allah and His Messenger know better." He said, "That was (angel) Gabriel. He came to teach you your religion."

Related by Muslim.

Themes

- Practicing Islamic etiquette
- Observing the pillars of Islam
- Believing in the foundations of faith (*arkān al-īmān*)
- Attaining excellence in worship (*iḥsān*)
- Signs preceding the Day of Judgment (*'alāmāt al-sā'ah*)

Explanation

This hadith is called the hadith of angel Gabriel (*Jibrīl*) as he appeared in the form of a human to Prophet Muhammad (pbuh) and his companions while they were sitting together. He came to teach them the essentials of their faith.

From the beginning of the hadith, there is an emphasis on manners as they come before everything else. Without them, good deeds cannot even be completed. Among the manners taught in the first part of the hadith is the way angel Gabriel was sitting in front of the teacher of humanity, Prophet Muhammad (pbuh). He demonstrated this by putting the palms of his hands on the Prophet's (pbuh) thighs and his knees against the Prophet's (pbuh) knees. Gabriel asked many questions and had the Prophet (pbuh) answer them, just as a student would do to his teacher. He did this to express his reverence to the Messenger of God (pbuh) and also to instruct others on how the spiritual teacher must be revered.

Prophet Muhammad (pbuh) further elaborates the favorable state (*maqām*) of the teacher or the scholar in the following statement, which is reported by Abū al-Dardā',

"إِنَّ الْعُلَمَاءَ وَرَثَةُ الأَنْبِيَاءِ".

"The learned are the heirs of the Prophets."[34]

Therefore, students and the general public should respect and honor their scholars by being cautious not to speak excessively in their presence

[34] Muhammad Ibn Hibban: *Sahih ibn Hibban*, Dar Ibn Hazm, Beirut, 2012, vol. 1, p. 550.

or belittle or criticize them, whether they are present or absent. They should avoid being passive or uncooperative, refrain from praising other scholars in front of them, and not burden them with too many questions. It is important not to raise their voices above the scholar's, engage in indecent talk, or display disrespectful behavior, such as extending their legs while sitting.

Not only in front of scholars, but Muslims, in general, are highly encouraged to exhibit the best ethics. That's because ethics or manners are strongly connected with belief. The Prophet (pbuh) emphasizes the importance of good manners in multiple statements. In a hadith reported by Abū Dāwūd, it is mentioned,

"أَكْمَلُ الْمُؤْمِنِينَ إِيمَانًا أَحْسَنُهُمْ خُلُقًا".

"Believers with the most completed faith are those who have the best manners"[35]

The Prophet's (pbuh) teachings on Islam and faith (*īmān*) stand as the fundamental principles of Islamic practice and belief. In this hadith, Prophet Muhammad (pbuh) concisely outlines Islam in five essential aspects: the Declaration of Faith (*shahādah*), prayer (*ṣalat*), charity (*zakāt*), fasting (*sawm*), and pilgrimage (*ḥajj*).[36] Regarding faith, he articulates it in six core beliefs: belief in God, His angels, His scriptures, His prophets, the Day of Judgment, and divine decree. These foundational pillars of Islam and faith are reiterated by the Prophet (pbuh) in several other hadiths, documented by various narrators.

Then the Prophet (pbuh) discussed a significant Islamic concept and practice known as "excellence" (*iḥsān*). In this hadith, he defined *iḥsān* as worshiping or serving Allah as if you see Him; even though you cannot see Him, know that He sees you. The Prophet (pbuh) emphasized the

---

[35] Abu Dawud al-Sijistani: *Sunan Abu Dawud*, Dar al-Risalah al-'Al-Alamiyyah, Damascus, 2009, vol. 7, Hadith no. 4682.

[36] More details on the pillars of Islam will be provided in the explanation of the third hadith.

importance of wholeheartedly performing worship with a deep awareness, striving to feel as though Allah is directly witnessed. If achieving this level of closeness is challenging, then maintaining awareness that Allah observes you suffices.

Some scholars consider *iḥsān* a spiritual state achievable through purifying one's ego with steadfast faith and righteous deeds. By overcoming selfish desires, one affirms the Oneness of God (*tawḥīd*) in their heart, focusing steadfastly on Allah, who observes them continually. This spiritual realization cultivates kindness and fosters benevolence towards all creation, marking *iḥsān* as a pinnacle of spiritual elevation. The Prophet (pbuh), through the arrangement of his words in the hadith, guides believers to understand that true faith and religious practices are paths to achieving this excellence (*iḥsān*), not merely confined to formal rituals. This perspective does not undermine Islamic formal rituals, nor does it suggest that one may abandon them upon achieving excellence. Instead, it emphasizes their role in deepening spiritual exploration and pursuit of goodness.

When commenting on the words of the Prophet (pbuh) about ihsān, Imam Saʿd al-Dīn ibn Masʿūd ibn ʿUmar al-Taftāzānī (d. 792/1390), in his commentary on the Forty Hadiths of Imam al-Nawawī, explains that ihsān denotes sincerity (*ikhlāṣ*) in religious practice. He further asserts that sincerity is crucial for validating one's faith and adherence to Islam; without sincere intention upon embracing Islam, subsequent good deeds may not solidify one's faith.[37]

Later in the hadith, Angel Gabriel asked Prophet Muhammad (pbuh) about the timing of the Day of Judgment. The Prophet's response emphasized that the one being questioned does not possess more knowledge about the end times than the one asking the question. This signifies that only Allah knows the exact timing of the world's culmination, concealed from His creation, as stated in the Qur'an:

"إِلَيْهِ يُرَدُّ عِلْمُ السَّاعَةِ"

---

[37] Sa'd al-Din Masud bin Umar bin Abd Allah: *Sharh al-Taftazani*, Dar al-Kutub al-Ilmiyyah, Beirut, 2004, p. 73.

"To him (alone) is attributed knowledge of the Hour."[38]

Angel Gabriel then inquired about the signs of the Last Day, to which the Prophet responded, "When the slave woman gives birth to her master." Hadith commentators have presented diverse interpretations of this phrase. Some suggest that it prophesies a societal decline in morals, reaching a point where children will mistreat their parents as if they were their own slaves or worse. Another interpretation, also mentioned by Imam Nawawī in his commentary on this hadith from *Ṣahiḥ Muslim* indicates a future scenario of societal chaos and familial breakdown. In this context, a wealthy young woman seeking to purchase a slave unwittingly buys her own mother instead.[39]

The Prophet (pbuh) then spoke of another sign of the Day of Judgment: seeing barefoot, destitute shepherds competing in the construction of tall buildings. This could symbolize villagers migrating to urban centers, gaining wealth quickly, and engaging in a race to build towering structures. We witness today how former shepherds from deserts and other remote regions move to cities, rapidly accumulate wealth, and compete in erecting skyscrapers.

After imparting these insights, Angel Gabriel departed. The Prophet (pbuh) informed ʿUmar and those present, "That was Gabriel. He came to teach you your religion."

---

[38] Q. (41:47).

[39] Muhyi al-Dīn Abu Zakariyya al-Nawawi: *Al-Minhaj fi Sharh Sahih Muslim ibn al-Hajjaj*, Dar al-Fikr al-Dawliyyah, Riyadh, no publication year, p. 82.

HADITH 3

الحديث الثالث

The Pillars of Islam

عَنْ أَبِي عَبْدِ الرَّحْمَنِ عَبْدِ اللَّهِ بْنِ عُمَرَ بْنِ الْخَطَّابِ رَضِيَ اللَّهُ عَنْهُمَا قَالَ:
سَمِعْت رَسُولَ اللَّهِ صلى الله عليه وسلم يَقُولُ:
"بُنِيَ الْإِسْلَامُ عَلَى خَمْسٍ: شَهَادَةِ أَنْ لَا إلَهَ إلا اللَّهُ وَأَنَّ مُحَمَّدًا رَسُولُ اللَّهِ، وَإِقَامِ الصَّلَاةِ، وَإِيتَاءِ الزَّكَاةِ، وَحَجِّ الْبَيْتِ، وَصَوْمِ رَمَضَانَ".
رواه البخاري ومسلم.

ʿAbdullāh, the son of ʿUmar (may God be pleased with both of them) said: I heard the Messenger of Allah, peace be upon him, say,

"Islam is built on five (pillars): testifying that there is no god but Allah, and that Muhammad is the messenger of Allah, and the establishment of prayer (*salat*), payment of the obligatory almsgiving (*zakat*), Pilgrimage to the House (Kaaba) and the fast of Ramadan."

Related by al-Bukhārī and Muslim.

Theme

- Islam is built on five pillars

Explanation

The five pillars outlined in this hadith are the practical foundations of Islam, as mentioned in the previous hadith. These pillars are established in the Qur'an through numerous verses, underscoring their importance for every Muslim. To be a true adherent of Islam, one must practice these pillars with full conviction. Neglecting the last four pillars without a valid excuse renders one sinful, while outright rejection of any or all of them takes one out of the fold of Islam.

The first pillar mentioned in this hadith is the very core of Islam: the Declaration (*shahādah*) of faith, which one must utter to become a Muslim. This declaration, "I declare there is no god but Allah, and I declare that Muhammad is the Messenger of Allah and His servant (*Ash-hadu an lā ilāha il-lallāh, wa ash-hadu anna Muhammadan ʿabduhu wa rasūluhu*)," must be uttered and made with full conviction and sincerity by those embracing Islam.

Muslims recite the declaration of faith in their prayers and are encouraged by the Prophet (pbuh) to repeat it daily. The *shahādah* holds numerous virtues and fascinating dimensions.

Regarding its virtues, Prophet Muhammad (pbuh) emphasized that the first part of the shahādah was not a new invention but had been proclaimed by previous prophets as well. In a hadith reported by the companion Ṭalhah bin ʿUbaydillāh bin Karīz, the Messenger of God (pbuh) stated,

"أَفْضَلُ الدُّعَاءِ يَوْمَ عَرَفَةَ، وَأَفْضَلُ مَا قُلْتُ أَنَا وَالنَّبِيُّونَ مِنْ قَبْلِي: قَوْلُ لا إِلَهَ إِلا اللَّهُ وَحْدَهُ لا شَرِيكَ لَهُ".

"The best supplication is the one performed during the day of ʿArafāt, and the most virtuous word mentioned by me and other prophets before me is: There is no god but Allah, one and only, without a partner."[40]

---

40 Malik ibn Anas: *Al-Muwatta*, Dar al-Turath al-Arabi, Beirut, 1985, p. 214-215.

Also, in another hadith it is reported that the Prophet (pbuh) told to his companion Abū Dharr al-Ghiffārī,

قَالَ أَبُو ذَرٍّ رَضِيَ اللَّهُ عَنْهُ: أَتَيْتُ النَّبِيَّ صَلَّى اللَّهُ عَلَيْهِ وَسَلَّمَ وَعَلَيْهِ ثَوْبٌ أَبْيَضُ وَهُوَ نَائِمٌ ثُمَّ أَتَيْتُهُ وَقَدْ اسْتَيْقَظَ فَقَالَ: "مَا مِنْ عَبْدٍ قَالَ لَا إِلَهَ إِلَّا اللَّهُ ثُمَّ مَاتَ عَلَى ذَلِكَ إِلَّا دَخَلَ الْجَنَّةَ قُلْتُ وَإِنْ زَنَى وَإِنْ سَرَقَ قَالَ وَإِنْ زَنَى وَإِنْ سَرَقَ قُلْتُ وَإِنْ زَنَى وَإِنْ سَرَقَ قَالَ وَإِنْ زَنَى وَإِنْ سَرَقَ قُلْتُ وَإِنْ زَنَى وَإِنْ سَرَقَ قَالَ وَإِنْ زَنَى وَإِنْ سَرَقَ عَلَى رَغْمِ أَنْفِ أَبِي ذَرٍّ وَكَانَ أَبُو ذَرٍّ إِذَا حَدَّثَ بِهَذَا قَالَ وَإِنْ رَغِمَ أَنْفُ أَبِي ذَرٍّ".

"There is no servant (of God) who passes away saying, 'There is no god but Allah' and does not enter Paradise." Abū Dharr asked the Prophet (pbuh), "Even if the person committed adultery and has stolen before?" He said, "Even if the person committed adultery and has stolen before." Abū Dhar repeated the question four times and he received the same answer from the Prophet (pbuh) with the addition of the Prophet (pbuh) on the fourth, "Even if it means the nose of Abū Dhar is rubbed in the dust." Whenever Abū Dhar would recount this (conversation with the Prophet (pbuh)), he would say: "Even if it means the nose of Abū Dharr is rubbed in the dust."[41]

This hadith clearly highlights not only the significance of expressing the word of Oneness of God, but also affirms that this declaration was mentioned by other Prophets as well. Abū Dharr was astonished by the response, as adultery and theft are among the major sins that carry severe punishments. However, through this hadith, the Prophet (pbuh) illustrates that a believer's departure from this world with full faith can atone for previous sins, even if they are significant. This is because someone who remains connected to God during the most challenging moments of their life has earned Allah's mercy and approval. Repentance is not explicitly mentioned, as it is implied, since one cannot be a true servant and devotee

---

[41] Muslim ibn al-Hajjaj: Sahih Muslim, Dar al-Tayyibah, Riyadh, 2006, vol. 1, p. 56.

of God without repenting. The saying: "Even if it means the nose of Abū Dharr is rubbed in the dust" stands for: whether Abū Dharr finds it easy to accept it or not, the truth remains.

The benefits of repeatedly saying the phrase "*Lā ilāha il-lāll-llāh*" are many, but the most significant one is the spiritual benefit and the profound sense of God's presence that a person feels when they recite it with sincerity, either in their heart or aloud. The question arises: Why is this phrase so special? The answer lies in its deep spiritual practice. When a person continually engages their heart and other spiritual faculties by repeating the Word of Unification, their inner being can be cleansed of everything but Allah Almighty. At this elevated spiritual state, they can experience the presence of God intimately, and Allah becomes their sole focus.

The Word of Unification starts with negation, "there is no god" (*lā ilāha*), followed by affirmation, "except Allah" (*il-lall-llāh*). Initially, the believer empties their spiritual components of all attachments to creation through negation (*lā ilāha*). Once they rid themselves of these material tendencies, their spiritual realm is dominated by Allah alone.

To attain this spiritual state, believers must strive to deepen their understanding of their Creator by engaging with the verses of the Qur'an, the sayings of Prophet Muhammad (pbuh), and the teachings of scholars and the righteous. Additionally, to enhance their comprehension of God, believers are encouraged to reflect on the nature and signs present in creation. Everything in existence serves as evidence of God's presence.

The importance of recognizing God's Oneness and understanding His Unity (as far as humanly possible) is also highlighted by Imam ʿAlī bin ʿUthmān al-Hujwīrī (d. 464/1071), who said: "The unification of God involves affirming this unification and possessing complete knowledge about it."[42]

Allah created humans with an innate tendency towards recognizing His Unity. Thus, it is natural for humans to accept and testify to God as the Creator of everything. Humans inherently seek to unify their

---

[42] Ali bin Uthman al-Hujwiri: *Kashf al-Mahjub*, translated from Persian to English by Reynold A. Nicholson, E.J.W. GIBB Memorial Trust, Wiltshire, England, 2000, p. 278.

understanding of the world. For instance, when they see leaves, roots, and fruits, they immediately think of the tree. When they observe light, feel warmth, and see rays, they instinctively think of the sun. Therefore, humans are naturally inclined to recognize unity. Similarly, when they perceive both the spiritual and physical realms, they should attribute them to one Creator, Allah Almighty.

The second pillar mentioned after the Declaration of Faith is the observance of prayer. The Messenger of Allah (peace and blessings be upon him) said in a hadith:

"رَأْسُ الْأَمْرِ الْإِسْلَامُ، وَعَمُودُهُ الصَّلَاةُ".

"The essence of this matter is Islam, and its pillar is prayer."[43]

In another well-known prophetic hadith, it is stated:

عن أَبِي هُرَيْرَةَ رضي الله عنه قَالَ: سَمِعْتُ رَسُولَ اللَّهِ صَلَّى اللَّهُ عَلَيْهِ وَسَلَّمَ يَقُولُ: "إِنَّ أَوَّلَ مَا يُحَاسَبُ بِهِ الْعَبْدُ يَوْمَ الْقِيَامَةِ مِنْ عَمَلِهِ صَلَاتُهُ فَإِنْ صَلُحَتْ فَقَدْ أَفْلَحَ وَأَنْجَحَ وَإِنْ فَسَدَتْ فَقَدْ خَابَ وَخَسِرَ".

Abū Hurayrah (r.a.) reported: I heard the Messenger of Allah (peace and blessings be upon him) say:

"The first deed for which a person will be called to account on the Day of Judgment is their prayer. If it is sound, they will be successful and saved. If it is deficient, they will have failed and be ruined…"[44]

The third pillar of Islam, mentioned by the Messenger of Allah (pbuh), is the giving of *zakāt*. The word "*zakāt*" comes from Arabic and has two main meanings: the first meaning is purification. A believer who gives *zakāt* purifies their wealth from what is forbidden and cleanses their heart from greed. The second meaning of *zakat* is growth. By giving *zakat*,

[43] This is part of Hadith 29 from this book.

[44] Al-Tirmidhi: *Jami' al-Tirmidhi*, vol. 1. p. 467.

the believer actually causes their wealth to increase in the long run, even though it might seem to decrease initially. The Messenger of Allah (pbuh) said in a hadith, "Wealth is not diminished by giving charity..."[45]

The fourth pillar of Islam, mentioned in the hadith, is the performance of Hajj. Every Muslim, male or female, is obligated to perform Hajj once in their lifetime if they meet certain conditions, such as being physically and financially able, being debt-free, and having reached the age of maturity.

Hajj, like some other Islamic rituals, is not an easy undertaking. The believer faces many challenges that must be overcome with patience. Additionally, during Hajj, the believer must perform the specified rituals with an understanding of their symbolism. These rituals help to enhance the believer's spiritual life and bring them closer to the Creator. For example, when a believer runs between the hills of Ṣafā and Marwā, they are reminded of lady Hājar's sacrifice for her son, Ismail. This act fosters greater empathy and care for mothers. It also leads the believer to a higher reality: that Allah cares for and loves His creation more than a mother loves her child.

When the believer completes all the Hajj rituals with full faith, devotion, and repentance to Allah, all their past sins are forgiven, and it is as if they are reborn. The Messenger of Allah (pbuh) said, "Whoever performs Hajj for the sake of Allah, without engaging in intimate relations or violating any Islamic laws, will return as if they were born anew."[46]

The final pillar of Islam, as mentioned by the Prophet of Allah (pbuh), is the fasting during the month of Ramadan. The word "*ṣawm*," which is translated as fasting, means to abstain from something, while in Islamic jurisprudence, it stands for abstaining from eating, drinking, and intimate relations from dawn until sunset.

The purpose of fasting in Islam is to achieve devotion and safeguard oneself from evil. The Qur'an states:

---

[45] Ahmad ibn Hanbal: *Musnad Ahmad ibn Hanbal*, Volume 2, page 315.

[46] Shamsuddin al-Kirmani: *Al-Kawakib al-Darari fī Sharh Sahih al-Bukhari*, vol. 8, p. 60.

"يَا أَيُّهَا الَّذِينَ آمَنُوا كُتِبَ عَلَيْكُمُ الصِّيَامُ كَمَا كُتِبَ عَلَى الَّذِينَ مِن قَبْلِكُمْ لَعَلَّكُمْ تَتَّقُونَ"

"O believers! Fasting is prescribed for you as it was prescribed for those before you, that you may become righteous."[47]

By abstaining for a short period from fulfilling physical needs, a believer prioritizes spiritual needs, resembling the heavenly beings—the angels—who always act following divine commands and are constantly engaged in the remembrance of God.

Imam Abū Hāmid Ghazālī (d. 505/1111), in his famous book *Iḥyā' 'Ulum al-Dīn*, writes about the inner dimensions of Islamic worship, particularly fasting, and explains that fasting is divided into three types:

1. Ordinary fasting (*ṣawm al-ʿumūm*): This type of fasting is practiced by many people and is merely abstaining from food, drink, and intimate relations.
2. Fasting of the elite (*ṣawm al-khūṣūṣ*): This type of fasting is observed by those who keep the ears, eyes, tongue, hands, feet, and all other organs away from sin.
3. Fasting of the elite of the elite (*ṣawm khuṣūṣ al-khuṣūṣ*): This refers to the category of those who fast with their hearts, abstaining from unworthy and irrelevant worldly thoughts, and withdrawing from everything except Allah.[48]

The one who fasts only by staying hungry and thirsty while not restraining from desires does not achieve the objective of Ramadan. Therefore, a believer must carefully control their tongue, eyes, and ears.

In his book *Sharḥ al-Taftazānī ʿalā al-Arbaʿīn al-Nawawiyyah*, the author Saʿd al-Dīn Masʿūd bin ʿUmar bin ʿAbdullāh (d. 792/1390), known as Imam Al-Taftazānī, it is cited that fasting is abstaining from the

---

[47] Q. (2:183).

[48] Abu Hamid Ghazali: Ihya Ulum al-Din, Dar al-Ma'rifah, Beirut, 1982, vol. 1, p. 234.

forbidden. This fasting is broken by indulging in what Allah (SWT) has permitted. However, a higher level of spiritual fasting is when a believer begins the fast by staying away from material things and breaks it by constantly maintaining a connection with the Divine Presence, God.[49]

---

[49] Sa'd al-Din Masud ibn Umar ibn Abdullah: *Sharh al-Taftazani ala al-Arbain al-Nawawiyyah*, p. 80.

HADITH 4

الحديث الرابع

The Creation of Man and His Future

عَنْ عَبْدِ اللهِ بنِ مَسْعُوْدْ رَضِيَ اللهُ عَنْهُ قَالَ: حَدَّثَنَا رَسُوْلُ اللهِ صلى الله عليه وسلم وَهُوَ الصَّادِقُ المَصْدُوْقُ:

"إِنَّ أَحَدَكُمْ يُجْمَعُ خَلْقُهُ فِيْ بَطْنِ أُمِّهِ أَرْبَعِيْنَ يَوْماً نُطْفَةً، ثُمَّ يَكُوْنُ عَلَقَةً مِثْلَ ذَلِكَ، ثُمَّ يَكُوْنُ مُضْغَةً مِثْلَ ذَلِكَ، ثُمَّ يُرْسَلُ إِلَيْهِ المَلَكُ فَيَنفُخُ فِيْهِ الرّوْحَ، وَيُؤْمَرُ بِأَرْبَعِ كَلِمَاتٍ: بِكَتْبِ رِزْقِهِ وَأَجَلِهِ وَعَمَلِهِ وَشَقِيٌّ أَوْ سَعِيْدٌ. فَوَالله الَّذِي لاَ إِلَهَ غَيْرُهُ إِنَّ أَحَدَكُمْ لَيَعْمَلُ بِعَمَلِ أَهْلِ الجَنَّةِ حَتَّى مَا يَكُوْنُ بَيْنَهُ وَبَيْنَهَا إِلاذِرَاعٌ فَيَسْبِقُ عَلَيْهِ الكِتَابُ فَيَعْمَلُ بِعَمَلِ أَهْلِ النَّارِ فَيَدْخُلُهَا، وَإِنَّ أَحَدَكُمْ لَيَعْمَلُ بِعَمَلِ أَهْلِ النَّارِ حَتَّى مَايَكُونُ بَيْنَهُ وَبَيْنَهَا إِلا ذِرَاعٌ فَيَسْبِقُ عَلَيْهِ الكِتَابُ فَيَعْمَلُ بِعَمَلِ أَهْلِ الجَنَّةِ فَيَدْخُلُهَا".

رواه البخاري ومسلم.

On the authority of ʿAbdullāh ibn Masʿūd (r.a.), who said: The Messenger of Allah (peace and blessings of Allah be upon him), and he is the truthful, the believed, narrated to us,

"Verily the creation of each one of you is brought together in his mother's womb for forty days in the form of a drop, then he becomes a clot of blood for a like period, then a morsel of flesh for a like period, then there is sent to him the angel who blows his soul into him and who is commanded with four matters: to write down his sustenance, his life span, his actions, and whether he will be happy or unhappy (i.e., whether he/she will be from the dwellers of Paradise or not). By the One, other than Whom there is no deity, verily one of you performs the actions of the people of Paradise until there is but an arm's length between him and it, and that which has been written overtakes him, and so he acts with the actions of the people of the Hellfire and thus enters it; and verily one of you performs the actions of the people of the Hellfire, until there is but an arm's length between him and it, and that which has been written overtakes him and so he acts with the actions of the people of Paradise and thus he enters it."

Related by al-Bukhārī and Muslim.

Themes

- Stages of human creation in the mother's womb
- The positive energy influencing humans in the Hereafter

Explanation

In the first part of this hadith, Prophet Muhammad (pbuh) describes the intricate stages of human creation. Remarkably, modern laboratory equipment has confirmed the accuracy of his words. Given that such detailed knowledge was unattainable with the technology available 1400 years ago, this statement by the Messenger of Allah (pbuh) is considered a prophetic miracle. Similar detailed explanations of a child's formation in the mother's womb are found in the Qur'an, where it states,

"وَلَقَدْ خَلَقْنَا الإِنسَانَ مِن سُلَالَةٍ مِّن طِينٍ. ثُمَّ جَعَلْنَاهُ نُطْفَةً فِي قَرَارٍ مَّكِينٍ. ثُمَّ خَلَقْنَا النُّطْفَةَ عَلَقَةً فَخَلَقْنَا الْعَلَقَةَ مُضْغَةً فَخَلَقْنَا الْمُضْغَةَ عِظَامًا فَكَسَوْنَا الْعِظَامَ لَحْمًا ثُمَّ أَنشَأْنَاهُ خَلْقًا آخَرَ فَتَبَارَكَ اللَّهُ أَحْسَنُ الْخَالِقِينَ"

"Man We did create from a quintessence (of clay); Then We placed him as (a drop of) sperm in a place of rest, firmly fixed; Then We made the sperm into a clot of congealed blood; then of that clot We made a (fetus) lump; then We made out of that lump bones and clothed the bones with flesh; then We developed out of it another creature. So blessed be Allah, the best to create!"[50]

These verses, along with the hadith, help readers understand that after certain phases, the baby becomes a complete human with a soul while still in the mother's womb. They also provide a basis for the prohibition of abortion after the soul enters the body, unless the mother's life is at risk.

The hadith further explains that before the baby is born, precisely right after the soul is instilled into the body, an angel is assigned to record the events pertaining to the baby's destiny. Some might interpret this as indicating that humans are prisoners of a predestined fate, determined before birth. This misunderstanding leads to a significant error in Islamic belief.

The answer lies in the sixth pillar of Islamic faith, which is belief in Divine Will and Decree (*qaḍā* and *qadar*). Humans are not created as robots; God has endowed them with free will to make different choices in life. However, God, in His omniscience, knows the decisions humans will make even before they are born. Therefore, He has decreed that everything be written down in the Preserved Tablet (*lawḥ al-maḥfūdh*). These decrees, unknown to man, are revealed to the angels who record them in their registers.

According to the hadith, it is crucial to understand that one should not despair, thinking that a sinful life makes entering Paradise impossible. Anyone can turn to Allah, seek His guidance, and experience a life filled with blessings and faith. Conversely, those guided by Islam must remain disciplined in their religious practices. Otherwise, a person on the verge of entering Paradise may fall into sin and end up among the inhabitants of Hell if they lose their connection with the Creator, oppose His teachings, and lose faith.

---

[50] Q. (23:12-4).

HADITH 5

الحديث الخامس

Avoiding Sin and Innovation

عَنْ أُمِّ الْمُؤْمِنِينَ أُمِّ عَبْدِ اللَّهِ عَائِشَةَ رَضِيَ اللَّهُ عَنْهَا، قَالَتْ: قَالَ: رَسُولُ اللَّهِ (صَلَّى اللَّهُ عَلَيْهِ وَآلِهِ وَسَلَّمَ): "مَنْ أَحْدَثَ فِي أَمْرِنَا هَذَا مَا لَيْسَ مِنْهُ فَهُوَ رَدٌّ".
وَفِي رِوَايَةٍ لِمُسْلِمٍ: "مَنْ عَمِلَ عَمَلًا لَيْسَ عَلَيْهِ أَمْرُنَا فَهُوَ رَدٌّ".
رَوَاهُ الْبُخَارِيُّ وَمُسْلِمٌ.

On the authority of the Mother of the Faithful, ʿĀishah (may Allah be pleased with her), who said: The Messenger of Allah (peace and blessings of Allah be upon him) said,

"He who innovates something in this matter of ours (i.e., Islam) that is not of it will have it rejected (by Allah)."

In one version by Muslim it reads: "He who does an act which we have not commanded, will have it rejected (by Allah)."

Related by al-Bukhārī and Muslim.

Theme

- Upholding the Islamic teachings

Explanation

Many scholars have stated that this hadith, along with the first hadith of this book, encapsulates the essence of Islam. The first hadith guides believers to be sincere in their intentions, while this hadith emphasizes the importance of performing deeds in accordance with Islamic teachings, as only then will such deeds be accepted.[51]

Islam is a complete way of life, perfected by God, as stated in the Qur'an:

"الْيَوْمَ أَكْمَلْتُ لَكُمْ دِينَكُمْ وَأَتْمَمْتُ عَلَيْكُمْ نِعْمَتِي وَرَضِيتُ لَكُمُ الْإِسْلَامَ دِينًا"

"This day I have perfected for you your religion and completed My favor upon you and have approved for you Islam as religion."[52]

Therefore, any new practice introduced into Islam that is claimed to be essential or obligatory, without basis in the Qur'an or prophetic tradition (*sunnah*), should be rejected.

It is also important to note that some people misuse this hadith to condemn others, labeling them as innovators or even nonbelievers simply because their practices do not fit within a particular interpretation of their "pure" understandings. This approach fosters division and enmity. The correct understanding of this hadith is that any new practice introduced into Islam as a religious ritual without having foundation in the Islamic primary sources should be rejected.

For example, introducing a new prayer (*ṣalāh*) alongside the five daily prayers, without basis in the mentioned sources, would be considered a bad innovation and should be rejected. However, holding a daily class to learn the science of *tajwīd* (rules of reading) is not a bad innovation harmful to the individual and community. While reading the Qur'an with *tajwīd* is obligatory for those capable, though there is no evidence that

---

[51] You can refer to the explanation by Ibn Hajar al-Asqalani: *Fath al-Bari Sharh Sahih al-Bukhari*, Dar al-Rayyan, Cairo, 1986, Volume 5, p. 357, Hadith 2550.

[52] Q. (5:3).

the Prophet (pbuh) or his companions held daily or weekly *tajwīd* classes. As long as such classes are not seen as a religious obligation, they do not constitute a bad innovation in Islam. Similarly, when a group gathers for virtuous or permissible (*mubāh*) activities, it is not considered harmful in religion, provided these activities are not viewed as religious practices when there is no proof in the Islamic sources.

HADITH 6

الحديث السادس

Guarding the Heart

عَنْ أَبِي عَبْدِ اللَّهِ النُّعْمَانِ بْنِ بَشِيرٍ رَضِيَ اللَّهُ عَنْهُمَا، قَالَ: سَمِعْتُ رَسُولَ اللَّهِ صلى الله عليه و سلم يَقُولُ:

"إنَّ الْحَلَالَ بَيِّنٌ، وَإِنَّ الْحَرَامَ بَيِّنٌ، وَبَيْنَهُمَا أُمُورٌ مُشْتَبِهَاتٌ لَا يَعْلَمُهُنَّ كَثِيرٌ مِنْ النَّاسِ، فَمَنْ اتَّقَى الشُّبُهَاتِ فَقْد اسْتَبْرَأَ لِدِينِهِ وَعِرْضِهِ، وَمَنْ وَقَعَ فِي الشُّبُهَاتِ وَقَعَ فِي الْحَرَامِ، كَالرَّاعِي يَرْعَى حَوْلَ الْحِمَى يُوشِكُ أَنْ يَرْتَعَ فِيهِ، أَلَا وَإِنَّ لِكُلِّ مَلِكٍ حِمًى، أَلَا وَإِنَّ حِمَى اللَّهِ مَحَارِمُهُ، أَلَا وَإِنَّ فِي الْجَسَدِ مُضْغَةً إذَا صَلَحَتْ صَلَحَ الْجَسَدُ كُلُّهُ، وَإِذَا فَسَدَتْ فَسَدَ الْجَسَدُ كُلُّهُ، أَلَا وَهِيَ الْقَلْبُ".

رَوَاهُ الْبُخَارِيُّ وَمُسْلِمٌ.

On the authority of an-Nu'mān ibn Bashīr (r.a.), who said: I heard the Messenger of Allah (pbuh) say,

"That which is lawful is clear and that which is unlawful is clear, and between the two of them are doubtful matters about which many people do not know. Thus, he who avoids doubtful matters clears himself in regard to his religion and his honor, but he who falls into doubtful matters (eventually) falls into that which is unlawful, like the shepherd who pastures around a sanctuary, all but grazing therein. Truly every king has a sanctuary, and truly Allah's sanctuary is His prohibitions. Truly in the body there is a morsel of flesh, which, if it be whole, all the body is whole, and which, if it is diseased, all of (the body) is diseased. Truly, it is the heart."

Related by al-Bukhārī and Muslim.

Themes

- Clarifying the permissible and forbidden in Islam
- Consequences of engaging in suspicious deeds
- The human heart

Explanation

Islam strongly emphasizes the importance of maintaining discipline and moral conduct. Numerous passages in the Qur'an and Hadith highlight the significance of abstaining from prohibitions and engaging in good deeds. These actions impact not only our worldly life but also our fate in the Hereafter. For example, Islam prohibits intoxicants.[53] Consuming such substances not only risks one's health in this life but one also may face severe consequences in the Hereafter.

In this hadith, there are also instructions on matters considered suspicious. Prophet Muhammad (pbuh), through his simple yet significant examples of suspicious deeds, advises believers to avoid actions with uncertain outcomes or unclear moral standing.

Muslim scholars hold various perspectives on the ruling of doubtful matters (*mushtabihāt*). Some view them as prohibited, others as permissible, and still others suggest they are neither clearly lawful nor unlawful. The latter group encourages believers to avoid these matters, akin to a shepherd who grazes near a preserve, risking overstepping its boundaries.

---

[53] Please see the ayah from the Qur'an, "O you who have believed, indeed, intoxicants, gambling, (sacrificing on) stone altars (to other than Allah), and divining arrows are but defilement from the work of Satan, so avoid it that you may be successful." Q. (5:90).

Imam Taqī al-Dīn Abū al-Fat-ḥ Muḥammad b.ʿAlī (d. 702/1302), commonly known as Ibn Daqīq al-ʿĪd, in his commentary on Imam al-Nawawī's Forty Hadiths, categorizes doubtful matters into three types:

1. When a person knows an action or item is essentially prohibited (*harām*) but doubts its status due to changed circumstances. For instance, if one is unsure whether meat has been slaughtered according to Islamic law, the prohibition remains until certainty is achieved.

2. When a person knows an action or item is permissible but doubts its status due to new circumstances. For example, doubting the validity of a divorce (*talāq*) declaration. These matters remain lawful unless proven otherwise.

3. When a person is uncertain about the permissibility or prohibition of an action or item with no clear guidance. In such cases, Imam Ibn Daqīq advises abstaining, similar to Prophet Muhammad (pbuh) refraining from eating a fallen date out of concern it might be charity.[54]

In this hadith, the Prophet (pbuh) also addresses the human heart when discussing forbidden, lewd, and suspicious deeds. Though he mentions the physical heart, he indicates the metaphysical one, which is emphasized in the Qur'an: "The Day when neither wealth nor children will benefit, but only one who comes to Allah with a sound heart."[55]

Mystical Islamic scholars have given special attention to the metaphysical heart (*qalb*). In the book *Sufism: A Wayfarer's Guide and Naqshbandi Way* by Emīn al-Al-Dīn al-Naqshbandī (d. 1410/1990), the heart is described as the center of Sufi knowledge and spiritual progress. Cleansing the heart of flaws is essential, allowing it to be filled with the Light of Almighty God and devoted to the remembrance of Allah (*dhikr*).[56]

---

[54] Ibn Daqiq Al-Id: *A Treasury of Hadith; A Commentary on Nawawi's Selection of Forty Prophetic Traditions,* trans. by Mokrane Guezzou, Kube Puplishing, Leicestershire, UK, 2016, p. 40.

[55] Q. (26:88-89).

[56] Amin Alauddin an-Naqshbandi: *Sufism, A Wayfarer's Guide to the Naqshbandi Way,* translated from Arabic to English by Muhtar Holland, Louisville, 2011, pp. 191-192.

The connection between permissible, forbidden, and suspicious deeds and the heart lies in their spiritual impact. Good deeds bring happiness and tranquility (*sakīnah*), while bad deeds cause despair and pain. The human heart perceives and is affected by these actions, which is why the Prophet (pbuh) emphasizes the heart's influence at the end of the hadith.

HADITH 7

الحَدِيث السَّابِع

Religion is Sincere Advice

عَنْ أَبِي رُقَيَّةَ تَمِيمِ بْنِ أَوْسٍ الدَّارِيِّ ❋ أَنَّ النَّبِيَّ (صَلَّى اللّهُ عَلَيْهِ وَآلِهِ وَسَلَّمَ) قَالَ: "الدِّينُ النَّصِيحَةُ. قُلْنَا: لِمَنْ؟ قَالَ لِلّهِ، وَلِكِتَابِهِ، وَلِرَسُولِهِ، وَلِأَئِمَّةِ الْمُسْلِمِينَ وَعَامَّتِهِمْ".

رَوَاهُ مُسْلِمٌ.

On the authority of Tamīm ibn Aws al-Dārī (r.a.): the Prophet (pbuh) said,

"The *dīn* (religion) is *naṣīḥah* (advice, sincerity)." We said "To whom?" He (peace and blessings of Allah be upon him) said, "To Allah, His Book, His Messenger, and to the leaders of the Muslims and their common folk."

Related by Muslim.

Themes

- Advice in Islam

Explanation

This hadith highlights a fundamental theme in Islam: advice (*al-*

naṣīḥa). The importance of advice is so central that Islam is closely identified with it, much like the significance of standing at ʿArafāt during pilgrimage. Providing and receiving advice is a major aspect of Islamic practice. What sets Muslims apart from followers of other beliefs is their mutual encouragement to perform good deeds and avoid evil actions. Allah describes Muslims in the Qur'an as: "You are the best nation produced (as an example) for mankind. You enjoin what is right and forbid what is wrong and believe in Allah..." (3:110).

Regarding the categories for which believers should exchange advice, the renowned Moroccan scholar Aḥmad al-Zarrūq (d. 899/1493) devoted an entire book to explaining this hadith. He states,

1. Advice for Allah: This is accomplished by following His instructions, supporting His religion, and submitting to His law.
2. Advice for His Messenger (pbuh): This involves following the Prophet's (pbuh) tradition, respecting his family, and showing compassion to all Muslims.
3. Advice for His Book (Qur'an): This is achieved by reflecting on its verses, adhering to its commands, and improving one's recitation.
4. Advice for the Muslim community: This includes honoring them, respecting their sanctity, and helping them in any situation.
5. Advice for the Muslim leaders (elite): This involves submitting to their rules (except those that conflict with Islam), approving their actions (unless they contradict Islamic knowledge), and assisting the needy without disdain.

It is crucial not only to give advice but also to accept it. The above explanation illustrates the comprehensive nature of counsel in Islam, involving Allah, His Book, His Messenger, the elite believers, and the general Muslim community. This hadith is also found in various other related narrations.

HADITH 8

الحديث الثامن

The Dignity of the Believer

عَنْ ابْنِ عُمَرَ رَضِيَ اللَّهُ عَنْهُمَا، أَنَّ رَسُولَ اللَّهِ (صَلَّى اللّهُ عَلَيْهِ وَآلِهِ وَسَلَّمَ) قَالَ:
"أُمِرْتُ أَنْ أُقَاتِلَ النَّاسَ حَتَّى يَشْهَدُوا أَنْ لَا إلَهَ إلَّا اللَّهُ وَأَنَّ مُحَمَّدًا رَسُولُ اللَّهِ، وَيُقِيمُوا الصَّلَاةَ، وَيُؤْتُوا الزَّكَاةَ؛ فَإِذَا فَعَلُوا ذَلِكَ عَصَمُوا مِنِّي دِمَاءَهُمْ وَأَمْوَالَهُمْ إلَّا بِحَقِّ الْإِسْلَامِ، وَحِسَابُهُمْ عَلَى اللَّهِ تَعَالَى".
رَوَاهُ الْبُخَارِيُّ وَمُسْلِمٌ.

On the authority of Abdullah ibn ʿUmar (r.a.), that the Messenger of Allah (peace and blessings of Allah be upon him) said:

"I have been ordered to fight against the people until they testify that there is none worthy of worship except Allah and that Muhammad is the Messenger of Allah, and until they establish the *salāh* and pay the *zakat*. And if they do that then they will have gained protection from me for their lives and property, unless (they commit acts that are punishable) in Islam, and their reckoning will be with Allah."

Related by al-Bukhārī and Muslim.

Themes

- The importance of spreading the core message of Islam: The Unity of Allah (*Tawḥīd*)
- Establishing justice among believers

Explanation

Before exploring the two themes of this hadith, it is crucial to analyze its first part: "I have been commanded to fight against people until they testify that there is no god but Allah…" If taken out of context, this statement may seem to contradict Qur'anic teachings and numerous prophetic sayings that prohibit forcing others to accept Islam. Unfortunately, some individuals, by misinterpreting this hadith and taking it out of context, have acted violently, while others have wrongfully accused Islam of being a religion of violence.

A linguistic analysis from the Qur'an, which was revealed in pure Arabic, shows that the term "*al-nās*," commonly translated as "people," can refer to all people, specific individuals, or social groups.[57] For example, in the Qur'an, it is said,

"They said to them: 'The idolaters[58] have gathered against you, so fear them.' But it (only) increased them in faith, and they said: 'Sufficient for us is Allah, and (He is) the best Disposer of affairs.'"[59]

Just as in the Qur'an, Prophet Muhammad (pbuh) also uses the term "*al-nās*" to specifically refer to idolaters. Scholars have noted that in

---

[57] Here, the word "*al-nās*" is mentioned, which in this context does not mean "all people" but "some people." According to some scholars of Qur'anic interpretation, it can also refer to a group of hypocrites instead of an individual or some individuals. For further reference, see: Muhammad Ibn Ahmed ibn Abi Bakr al-Qurtubi: *Jami' al-Ahkam al-Qur'an*, Mu'assasat al-Risalah, Damascus, 2006, vol. 5, p. 422.

[58] Again, here, in the Arabic language, the word "*al-nās*" is used, which stands for a specific group of people, social group, the idol worshippers.

[59] Q. (3:173).

the mentioned hadith, the Messenger of Allah (pbuh) addresses the idolaters. It can be understood as, "I have been ordered to fight against the idolaters."[60]

Why idolaters? Historical accounts of the Prophet's (pbuh) life reveal numerous instances where idolaters persecuted, tortured, and killed many of the Prophet's Companions and their families. They attempted to kill the Prophet (pbuh) and forced him and many believers to flee their homes. While the believers lived peacefully in Medina, idolaters repeatedly waged war against them, aiming to destroy the Prophet (pbuh), his message, and his followers. The Prophet (pbuh) was commanded by Allah to defend against them: "Fight the idolaters collectively as they fight against you collectively. And know that Allah is with those who fear Him."[61]

Prophet Muhammad (pbuh) was ready to sacrifice everything to preserve and spread the ultimate truth: "There is no god but Allah, Muhammad is the Messenger of Allah." This message was fundamentally opposed to idolatry and the politics of idolaters. The Prophet (pbuh) and his followers were committed to safeguarding and disseminating this message without hindrance.

In the second part of the hadith, the Messenger of Allah (pbuh) emphasizes that anyone who accepts Islam and follows the path of Allah enjoys equal rights with all other members of the Muslim community.

---

[60] For further reference, see: Muhammad Ibn Hajar al-Asqalani: *Fath al-Bari*, Ihya al-Turath al-Arabi, Beirut, 1981, vol. 1, p. 64.

[61] Q. (9:36).

HADITH 9

الحديث التاسع

Obligations Are Proportional to Capability

عَنْ أَبِي هُرَيْرَةَ عَبْدِ الرَّحْمَنِ بْنِ صَخْرٍ ﵁ قَالَ: سَمِعْت رَسُولَ اللَّهِ (صَلَّى اللّهُ عَلَيْهِ وَآلِهِ وَسَلَّمَ) يَقُولُ:
"مَا نَهَيْتُكُمْ عَنْهُ فَاجْتَنِبُوهُ، وَمَا أَمَرْتُكُمْ بِهِ فَأْتُوا مِنْهُ مَا اسْتَطَعْتُمْ، فَإِنَّمَا أَهْلَكَ الَّذِينَ مِنْ قَبْلِكُمْ كَثْرَةُ مَسَائِلِهِمْ وَاخْتِلَافُهُمْ عَلَى أَنْبِيَائِهِمْ".
رَوَاهُ الْبُخَارِيُّ وَمُسْلِمٌ.

On the authority of Abū Hurayrah (r.a.) who said: I heard the Messenger of Allah (peace and blessings of Allah be upon him) say,

"What I have forbidden for you, avoid. What I have ordered you (to do), do as much of it as you can. For verily, it was only the excessive questioning and their disagreeing with their Prophets that destroyed (the nations) who were before you."

Related by al-Bukhārī and Muslim.

Themes

- Avoidance of prohibitions and adherence to what God has permitted
- The harm of unessential numerous questions and the consequences of opposing the Prophets

Explanation

Through this hadith, it is also important to emphasize that abandoning a forbidden action is more valuable than performing a good deed. The intention is not to diminish the rewards of good deeds; however, when compared, abstaining from a forbidden action yields a greater reward. Therefore, the hadith clarifies: "Stay away from those things which I have forbidden you, and do what you have been commanded as much as you can..."

A distinguishing characteristic of Muslims, compared to followers of other faiths, is their commitment to avoiding what God has prohibited. However, some individuals consider consuming non-halal meat as a forbidden act and refrain from it, yet they neglect to address negative traits such as lying, discord, and causing confusion among people. Similarly, others prioritize external prohibitions but overlook internal ones, such as slander, deceit, and betrayal, which can undermine one's virtuous deeds. Indeed, refraining from slander not only helps in avoiding sin but also serves as a pathway to attaining God's Paradise in the Hereafter. The Qur'an mentions,

"وَأَمَّا مَنْ خَافَ مَقَامَ رَبِّهِ وَنَهَى النَّفْسَ عَنِ الْهَوَى. فَإِنَّ الْجَنَّةَ هِيَ الْمَأْوَى"

"And as for the one who fears the position of his Lord and prevents the soul from (*unlawful*) inclination, then indeed, Paradise will be his refuge."[62]

In his famous book, Kitāb al-Luma', the great scholar Abū Naṣr al-Sarrāj (d. 378/988) mentions that the Islamic scholar Ibn Khubeyk said, "A person who fears his own ego (*nafs*) more than he fears the devil, I consider him as one who fears falling into mistakes."[63]

Regarding the avoidance of excessive questioning mentioned in that

---

[62] Q. (79:40-41).

[63] Abu Nasr al-Sarraj: *Kitab Luma'*, Dar al-Kutub al-Hadithah bi Misr, Cairo, 1960, p. 90.

hadith, Islam does not oppose questioning in general, but rather questions asked with ill intentions, provocatively, or those that are excessive and unnecessary. Excessive and unnecessary questions can lead to the beginning of doubt.

In fact, the Qur'an contains an entire chapter, the longest one, known as the "Chapter of the Cow" (Surah al-Baqarah). One of the significant events recounted in this chapter is the story of the people of Musa (pbuh) and the cow that Musa's (pbuh) followers were commanded to sacrifice. God would perform a miracle with its meat: placing it on the body of a dead person would bring the dead back to life and reveal the identity of their killer.[64]

The people began questioning Musa (pbuh) about which cow to sacrifice, including its color. However, God had not instructed them to delve into such specifics; rather, they were simply commanded to choose a cow and sacrifice it. The Qur'an mentions that due to their numerous questions and disobedience, they nearly failed to carry out the sacrifice.

The Messenger of Allah (pbuh) in a sound hadith transmitted by Ibn ʿAbbās (r.a.) mentions of the event: "It would have sufficed them to sacrifice any kind of cow, but they made it difficult for themselves, and Allah made it difficult for them."[65] This example illustrates the importance of limiting oneself from asking unnecessary questions.

---

64 See Q. (2:71).

65 Jalal al-Din al-Mahalli and Jalal al-Din al-Suyuti: *Tafsir al-Jalalayn*, al-Maktab al-Islami, Beirut, special edition by the Ministry of Religion for Islamic Affairs of the State of Qatar, no publishing year available, p. 11.

HADITH 10

الحديث العاشر

The Virtues of Adhering to the Lawful

عَنْ أَبِي هُرَيْرَةَ ﷺ قَالَ: قَالَ رَسُولُ اللَّهِ (صَلَّى اللَّهُ عَلَيْهِ وَآلِهِ وَسَلَّمَ):
"إِنَّ اللَّهَ طَيِّبٌ لَا يَقْبَلُ إِلَّا طَيِّبًا، وَإِنَّ اللَّهَ أَمَرَ الْمُؤْمِنِينَ بِمَا أَمَرَ بِهِ الْمُرْسَلِينَ
فَقَالَ تَعَالَى: 'يَا أَيُّهَا الرُّسُلُ كُلُوا مِنْ الطَّيِّبَاتِ وَاعْمَلُوا صَالِحًا'، وَقَالَ تَعَالَى: "يَا
أَيُّهَا الَّذِينَ آمَنُوا كُلُوا مِنْ طَيِّبَاتِ مَا رَزَقْنَاكُمْ" ثُمَّ ذَكَرَ الرَّجُلَ يُطِيلُ السَّفَرَ
أَشْعَثَ أَغْبَرَ يَمُدُّ يَدَيْهِ إِلَى السَّمَاءِ: يَا رَبِّ! يَا رَبِّ! وَمَطْعَمُهُ حَرَامٌ، وَمَشْرَبُهُ حَرَامٌ،
وَمَلْبَسُهُ حَرَامٌ، وَغُذِّيَ بِالْحَرَامِ، فَأَنَّى يُسْتَجَابُ لَهُ؟".
رَوَاهُ مُسْلِمٌ.

On the authority of Abū Hurayrah (r.a.) who said: The Messenger of Allah (pbuh) said,

"Allah the Almighty is Good and accepts only that which is good. And verily Allah has commanded the believers to do that which He has commanded the Messengers. So the Almighty has said: 'O (you) Messengers! Eat of the good and wholesome (food), and perform righteous deeds,'[66] and the Almighty has said: 'O you who believe! Eat of the lawful things that We have provided you.'"[67] Then he (pbuh) mentioned (the case) of a man who, having journeyed far, is disheveled and dusty, and

---

[66] Q. (23:51).

[67] Q. (2:172).

who spreads out his hands to the sky saying "O Lord! O Lord!," while his food is unlawful, his drink is unlawful, his clothing is unlawful, and he has been nourished unlawfully, so how can (his supplication) be answered?

Related by Muslim.

Theme

- The positive consequences that come as a result of steadfastness in what God has permitted

Explanation

The Qur'anic verse states, "Truly, Allah, the Exalted, is Good and does not accept other than good," and this hadith encourages believers to strike a balance between outward actions and internal virtues. This balance is clearly illustrated through the intertwined themes within the hadith. It discusses the consumption of good and permissible food, the performance of good deeds from the heart, and emphasizes the benevolence of the Creator. Food symbolizes superficial acts, while good deeds of the heart reflect deeper spiritual actions, and Allah's benevolence underscores His acceptance and reward for these deeds.

Additionally, the hadith mentions the phrase, "Allah commanded the believers just as He commanded the Messengers," indicating that good deeds, worship, and abstaining from prohibited matters were not directives solely for Prophets and Messengers, but for all of humanity. Therefore, it is incorrect for some to assert that these obligations were specific only to the Prophets, implying that as ordinary humans, we are incapable of emulating their conduct.

Muslims are urged by Allah Almighty to consistently emulate the example set by Prophet Muhammad (pbuh) throughout their lives. The Qur'an affirms,

"لَّقَدْ كَانَ لَكُمْ فِي رَسُولِ اللَّهِ أُسْوَةٌ حَسَنَةٌ لِّمَن كَانَ يَرْجُو اللَّهَ وَالْيَوْمَ الْآخِرَ وَذَكَرَ اللَّهَ كَثِيرًا"

"Indeed in the Messenger of Allah you have a good example to follow for him who hopes in Allah and the Last Day and remembers Allah much."[68]

The Creator's benevolence towards humanity is also evident in the diverse array of products He has provided for sustenance. Yet, many people overlook these blessings and opt for products that not only jeopardize their health but also impair their intellect. Compromising one's health diminishes their ability to fulfill religious and social duties. Simultaneously, impairing intellect through the consumption of alcohol, drugs, and other intoxicants distances individuals from their Creator, reducing their awareness of Him.

In this hadith, the Messenger of Allah (pbuh) also references the Qur'anic verse, "Eat of the good things We have provided for you."[69]

This verse underscores the consumption of pure and nutritious foods over processed ones that offer fewer health benefits. Such processed foods have been linked to various illnesses and premature deaths worldwide. In recent years, institutions of higher education and various organizations advocate for the use of natural products, which can prevent numerous diseases, including cancer.[70] Meanwhile, the Qur'an has emphasized the consumption of wholesome and pure foods for over 1400 years.

To clarify this hadith further, the Messenger of Allah (pbuh) concludes with an example, illustrating a person who consumes, dresses in, and drinks from the forbidden. Since Allah accepts only what is good, how can such a person's prayers be accepted? It is crucial to understand that

---

68 Q. (33:21).

69 Q. (7:160).

70 "Ultra-processed foods linked to increased cancer risk, diabetes, and heart disease," *World Cancer Research Fund International*, November 14, 2023, https://www.wcrf.org/news-events/ultra-processed-foods-linked-to-increased-cancer-risk-diabetes-and-heart-disease.

prohibitions for Muslims extend beyond pork, alcoholic beverages, and other explicitly forbidden substances. They also encompass items that are initially permissible but become prohibited due to unlawful acquisition methods, such as stealing a product—a transgression that not only involves theft but also its subsequent use.

HADITH 11

الحديث الحادي عشر

Steering Clear of Doubtful Matters

عَنْ أَبِي مُحَمَّدٍ الْحَسَنِ بْنِ عَلِيِّ بْنِ أَبِي طَالِبٍ سِبْطِ رَسُولِ اللَّهِ (صَلَّى اللّهُ عَلَيْهِ وَآلِهِ وَسَلَّمَ) وَرَيْحَانَتِهِ رَضِيَ اللَّهُ عَنْهُمَا قَالَ: حَفِظْت مِنْ رَسُولِ اللَّهِ (صَلَّى اللّهُ عَلَيْهِ وَآلِهِ وَسَلَّمَ):

"دَعْ مَا يُرِيبُك إلَى مَا لَا يُرِيبُك".

رَوَاهُ التِّرْمِذِيُّ، وَالنَّسَائِيّ، وَقَالَ التِّرْمِذِيُّ: حَدِيثٌ حَسَنٌ صَحِيحٌ.

On the authority of Abū Muḥammad al-Ḥasan ibn ʿAlī ibn Abī Tālib (r.a.), the grandson of the Messenger of Allah (pbuh) and the one much loved by him, who said: I memorized from the Messenger of Allah (pbuh),

"Leave that which makes you doubt for that which does not make you doubt."

Related by al-Tirmidhī and an-Nasāī. Al-Tirmidhī said that it was a reliable-authentic (*ḥasan sahīh*) hadith.

Theme

- Avoiding dubious activities prevents believers from falling into sin

Explanation

This hadith excerpt is part of the collection by Imam Al-Tirmidhī and Imam al-Nasāī. Its message is applicable to all individuals, with particular significance for devout believers. For newcomers to Islam, the initial focus should be on avoiding outright prohibitions, followed by a determined effort to avoid doubtful matters.

The profound lesson from this hadith underscores the importance for believers to prioritize avoiding doubtful thoughts in Islam, which often stem from the deceptive influence of the accursed devil. Satan endeavors to lead people astray from the righteous path by instilling doubts regarding God, angels, and the Day of Judgment. Those who resist the devil's temptations and shun his whisperings are guided by the Lord towards clarity and steadfastness. As the Qur'an affirms,

"إِنَّ الَّذِينَ اتَّقَوْا إِذَا مَسَّهُمْ طَائِفٌ مِّنَ الشَّيْطَانِ تَذَكَّرُوا فَإِذَا هُم مُّبْصِرُونَ"

"Indeed, those who fear Allah - when an impulse touches them from Satan, they remember (Him) and at once they have insight."[71]

[71] Q. (7:201).

HADITH 12

الحديث الثاني عشر

Avoiding What Does Not Concern You

عَنْ أَبِي هُرَيْرَةَ ۞ قَالَ: قَالَ رَسُولُ اللَّهِ (صَلَّى اللَّهُ عَلَيْهِ وَآلِهِ وَسَلَّمَ):
"مِنْ حُسْنِ إِسْلَامِ الْمَرْءِ تَرْكُهُ مَا لَا يَعْنِيهِ".
حَدِيثٌ حَسَنٌ، رَوَاهُ التِّرْمِذِيُّ، ابن ماجه.

On the authority of Abū Hurayrah (r.a.) who said: The Messenger of Allah (peace and blessings of Allah be upon him) said,

"Part of the perfection of one's Islam is his leaving that which does not concern him."

A reliable hadith which was related by al-Tirmidhī and others in this manner.

Theme

- Promoting a perfect Islamic character by focusing on what truly matters

Explanation

The Hadith is very short but contains a great message. Man is required to move away from what he does not belong to.

In Imam Nawawī's commentary on *Ṣaḥīḥ Muslim*, he highlights the insightful statement of ʿAbdullāh Ibn Abī Zayd, a renowned Moroccan scholar from the 10th century. This statement encapsulates the essence of all the sayings of Prophet Muhammad (pbuh) in four key hadiths, one of which emphasizes that "Part of the perfection of one's Islam is his leaving that which does not concern him."[72]

The negative consequences of humans worrying about matters that do not concern them can be numerous, with one of the most significant being the unnecessary waste of time.

Time is a gift from God for humans to use wisely. It serves as evidence through which individuals earn or forfeit rewards from their Creator. Therefore, wasting this precious gift on tasks that are not one's own responsibility represents a significant loss, for which individuals will be held accountable.

Consider having a sack of money and daily throwing large sums into a lake. This action is futile, resulting only in financial loss and future uncertainty. Similarly, wasting time by worrying about things that do not pertain to oneself is equally unproductive and devoid of benefit.

Dedicated believers maximize their time, understanding that their righteous efforts in this life yield rewards in the next world.

The example below illustrates the reverence for time among those close to God (*awliyā*). It is recounted that Ḥasan Bin Ṣinvān, seated on the first floor of a house, inquired about its construction date from its owner. It was a question deemed insignificant. Shortly after, he regretted this trivial inquiry, admonishing himself (*nafs*): "You are squandering your valuable time on trivial matters." As a result, he wept for nearly a year.[73] This example showcases the sensitivity of a person close to God who, despite not harming anyone or uttering anything absurd, felt remorse for asking something unnecessary.

---

[72] Ebi Abdullah al-Razi: *Mashaykhah Ebi Abdullah al-Razi*, Dar al-Hijrah, Riyadh, 1994, p. 196

[73] Abu Hamid al-Ghazali: *Minhaj al-Abidin*, Mu'assasat al-Risalah, 1st edition, Beirut, 1989, p. 139.

Today, people from different social backgrounds should ponder these examples, as many not only entangle themselves in matters beyond their concern but also inadvertently cause harm to others.

HADITH 13

الحديث الثالث عشر

Wishing for Others What You Wish for Yourself

عَنْ أَبِي حَمْزَةَ أَنَسِ بنِ مَالِكٍ ❀ خَادِمِ رَسُولِ اللَّهِ ❀ عَنِ النَّبِيِّ (صَلَّى اللّهُ عَلَيْهِ
وَآلِهِ وَسَلَّمَ) قَالَ:
"لاَ يُؤْمِنُ أَحَدُكُمْ حَتَّى يُحِبَّ لِأَخِيهِ مَا يُحِبُّ لِنَفْسِهِ".
رَوَاهُ الْبُخَارِيُّ وَمُسْلِمٌ.

On the authority of Abū Hamzah Anas bin Mālik (r.a.), the servant of the Messenger of Allah (pbuh), that the Prophet (pbuh) said,

"None of you (truly) believes until he loves for his brother that which he loves for himself."

Related by al-Bukhārī and Muslim.

Theme

- The care of a believer for others

Explanation

According to the scholar Abdullāh Ibn Ebī Zayd, this hadith is one of the four fundamental hadiths of Islamic morality, similar to the one before it.

The Messenger of Allah (pbuh) links altruism (*al-īthār*) with faith, highlighting the strong connection between belief and practice. In this hadith, the phrase "his brother" is mentioned. According to many scholars, the "brother of a believer" refers not only to a brother by blood but also to a brother in faith and humanity. For each of these three categories, the believer has specific obligations.

For his brother by blood, he must show love and respect, maintain close family ties, and more. For his brother in Islam, he is obliged to greet him, pray for him, help him, visit him, and so on. Regarding his brother in humanity, he should wish for him the same guidance that he desires for himself to be on the right path. All this is part of sacrifice and altruism toward others. The more a believer helps and sacrifices for others, the more happiness he will find in this world and the Hereafter.

The desire to love for others what you love for yourself is achieved by weakening the ego (*nafs*). When a person has a developed ego, his interest stops at himself, and he is so preoccupied with fulfilling his desires that he is almost unaware of what is happening around him. Although he occasionally shows interest in being close to others, it is often a hidden hypocrisy and a desire to convince himself and others that there are still pieces of goodness within him. In this state of distancing between the individual's heart and God, there stands a thick wall that does not fall except by weakening the ego.

Islamic history tells us that when the emigrants from Mecca arrived in Medina, the Prophet (pbuh) immediately established brotherhood between them. He did this with full conviction that brotherhood among believers is a primary impetus for maintaining community harmony. The fruits of this brotherhood are described in the Qur'an with these words:

"وَالَّذِينَ تبوؤوا الدَّارَ وَالْإِيمَانَ مِن قَبْلِهِمْ يُحِبُّونَ مَنْ هَاجَرَ إِلَيْهِمْ وَلَا يَجِدُونَ فِي صُدُورِهِمْ حَاجَةً مِّمَّا أُوتُوا وَيُؤْثِرُونَ عَلَى أَنفُسِهِمْ وَلَوْ كَانَ بِهِمْ خَصَاصَةٌ وَمَن يُوقَ شُحَّ نَفْسِهِ فَأُولَٰئِكَ هُمُ الْمُفْلِحُونَ"

"And those who, before them, had settled in the Home (i.e., al-Madinah) and had embraced the faith, love those who migrate to them and find not any want in their breasts for what they have been given but give them preference over themselves, even though they are in privation. And whoever is protected from the stinginess of his soul, it is those who will be the successful."[74]

[74] Q. (59:9).

HADITH 14

الحديث الرابع عشر

The Prohibition of Killing a Believer

عَنْ ابْنِ مَسْعُودٍ ❀ قَالَ: قَالَ رَسُولُ اللَّهِ (صَلَّى اللَّهُ عَلَيْهِ وَآلِهِ وَسَلَّمَ):
"لَا يَحِلُّ دَمُ امْرِئٍ مُسْلِمٍ إِلَّا بِإِحْدَى ثَلَاثٍ: الثَّيِّبُ الزَّانِي، والنَّفْسُ بِالنَّفْسِ،
وَالتَّارِكُ لِدِينِهِ الْمُفَارِقُ لِلْجَمَاعَةِ".
رَوَاهُ الْبُخَارِيُّ وَمُسْلِمٌ.

On the authority of Ibn Masood (r.a.) who said: The Messenger of
Allah (peace and blessings of Allah be upon him) said,

"It is not permissible to spill the blood of a Muslim except in three
(instances): the married person who commits adultery, a life for a life,
and the one who forsakes his religion and separates from the community."

Related by al-Bukhārī and Muslim.

Themes

- The importance of protecting the life of a believer
- Preserving the Muslim community from loss, division, and
destruction

Explanation

It is truly tragic what happened to Muslims in the 20th century and what continues to happen in the 21st century. Since the destruction of the last Islamic Caliphate, the Ottomans, the lives of Muslims around the world have been treated with greater disregard than many other groups. Their blood is spilled for personal interests, whether by non-Muslims or by those who claim to be Muslims but have nothing in common with Islam except the name.

The Prophet (pbuh) emphasized the importance of a believer's life by saying, "Abusing a believer is an evil act, and fighting (*qitāl*) against him is disbelief (in Allah)."[75] This statement indicates that fighting a believer is tantamount to disbelief in Allah, suggesting that killing a believer has even graver consequences.

In another part of the main hadith we are commenting on, the Messenger of Allah (pbuh) outlines the categories of those who, due to their crimes, are subject to capital punishment. This part of the hadith is often taken out of context, causing misunderstandings among those with a limited understanding of Islam and its objectives.

Islam fundamentally aims to establish sound morality, pure faith, and order in society. From the manner of prayer and spiritual education to interpersonal relationships and the treatment of animals and plants, Islam prescribes a unique discipline and sets boundaries that should not be crossed, as crossing them can lead to significant consequences. The preservation of these boundaries is encouraged not only by Islam but also by other faiths sharing similar principles, although such boundaries are often deemed outdated by many in modern societies.

Before explaining the three categories of people mentioned in this hadith, it is important to note that Islamic law (*sharia*) is based on preserving five essential principles (*al-ḍarūriy-yāt al-khams*), which are crucial for the security and development of a community.[76] One of these principles is the protection of human life. In fact, Islam goes even further,

---

[75] Muslim ibn al-Hajjaj: *Sahih Muslim*, p. 48.

[76] See Ahmed al-Raysuni: *Nadhariyyah al-Makasid inda al-Imam al-Shatibi*, Al-Maʿhad al-Alami li al-Fikr al-Islami,Hemdon, Virginia, 1995, p. 172.

emphasizing not only the protection of life but also its nurturing and development. The Qur'an states,

"وَمَنْ أَحْيَاهَا فَكَأَنَّمَا أَحْيَا النَّاسَ جَمِيعًا"

"...and whoever saves a life, it is as if he had saved all mankind."[77]

Regarding the first category mentioned in this hadith, a wise saying goes: "If morality leaves a people, the people themselves will disappear with it." Extramarital sexual relations between a man and a woman are severely punished in Islam because they contribute to moral decay in society. However, for the death penalty to be implemented, the act must be witnessed in explicit detail by at least four witnesses; otherwise, the punishment is not imposed.[78] This high level of scrutiny ensures that the act must be public or nearly public for it to be punishable, reflecting an effort to prevent moral corruption among people. Such penalties must be issued by an Islamic court and not through individual judgment and execution, a mistake that continues to be practiced in some remote places today.[79]

The hadith goes on to mention the second category of those who receive capital punishment: those who commit murder. The court-imposed death penalty for a person convicted of murder is a common practice in many countries, including Western ones. If a killing occurs in self-defense or unintentionally, other legal consequences may apply instead of the death penalty.[80]

Regarding the third category mentioned in this hadith, it has sparked significant controversy, particularly in the Western world, where it is often misunderstood and misinterpreted. This misinterpretation sometimes portrays Islam as a religion that allegedly does not respect religious

---

[77] Q. (5:32).

[78] See Badr al-Din al-Ayni al-Hanafi: *Al-Binayah Sharh al-Hidayah*, Dar al-Kutub al-Ilmiyyah, Beirut, 2000, vol. 6, p. 260.

[79] See Muhammad Ata Alsid Sidahmad: *The Hudud*, al-Basheer Publication, Malaysia, 1995, p. 118.

[80] See Badr al-Din al-Ayni al-Hanafi: *Binayah Sharh al-Hidayah*, vol. 13, p. 104.

freedom and individual rights in choosing faith. However, the Qur'an provides clear and unequivocal responses to such misconceptions,

"لَا إِكْرَاهَ فِي الدِّينِ قَد تَّبَيَّنَ الرُّشْدُ مِنَ الْغَيِّ"

"There is no compulsion in religion, for the right way is clearly distinguished from the wrong way..."[81]

Furthermore, the Qur'an states,

"وَقُلِ الْحَقُّ مِن رَّبِّكُمْ فَمَن شَاءَ فَلْيُؤْمِن وَمَن شَاءَ فَلْيَكْفُرْ"

"And say, 'The truth is from your Lord, so whoever wills, let him believe; and whoever wills, let him disbelieve.'"[82]

These and some other verses in the Qur'an clearly show that Islam is a faith accepted through belief in mind and heart, not through compulsion by force.

During the Prophet's (pbuh) time in the city of Medina, after the establishment of the Islamic state, there were hypocrites whose lack of faith the Prophet (pbuh) was aware of through the Qur'an. However, he never exposed them or took action against them, as they did not openly renounce Islam after having accepted it.[83] Those who left Islam at that time, and later, became enemies of Islam by joining forces opposing the Muslims. Such traitors posed a greater threat than ordinary enemies due to their extensive knowledge of the social, economic, military, and political conditions of the Muslims, which they would not hesitate to disclose to the enemies of Muslims. This act, known in modern terms as espionage, is punishable by death in many countries even in modern times.

In the life of the Prophet and his companions (may God be pleased with them all), we do not find examples of the Prophet (pbuh) investigating

---

81 Q (2:256).

82 Q. (18:29).

83 For further details, see the surah "The Hypocrites" (al-Munafiqun) in the Qur'an.

people's faith, nor fighting people of other faiths who didn't threaten him and his community. The Qur'an was clear in mentioning,

"لَّا يَنْهَاكُمُ ٱللَّهُ عَنِ ٱلَّذِينَ لَمْ يُقَٰتِلُوكُمْ فِى ٱلدِّينِ وَلَمْ يُخْرِجُوكُم مِّن دِيَٰرِكُمْ أَن تَبَرُّوهُمْ وَتُقْسِطُوٓاْ إِلَيْهِمْ ۚ إِنَّ ٱللَّهَ يُحِبُّ ٱلْمُقْسِطِينَ. إِنَّمَا يَنْهَاكُمُ ٱللَّهُ عَنِ ٱلَّذِينَ قَٰتَلُوكُمْ فِى ٱلدِّينِ وَأَخْرَجُوكُم مِّن دِيَٰرِكُمْ وَظَٰهَرُواْ عَلَىٰٓ إِخْرَاجِكُمْ أَن تَوَلَّوْهُمْ ۚ وَمَن يَتَوَلَّهُمْ فَأُوْلَٰٓئِكَ هُمُ ٱلظَّٰلِمُونَ"

"Allah does not forbid you from dealing kindly and fairly with those who have neither fought nor driven you out of your homes. Surely Allah loves those who are fair. Allah only forbids you from befriending those who have fought you for (your) faith, driven you out of your homes, or supported (others) in doing so. And whoever takes them as friends, then it is they who are the (true) wrongdoers."[84]

The Prophet (pbuh) advised people to show mercy to each other, emphasizing that those who do so will receive mercy from the Most Merciful. In another saying of the Prophet (pbuh), he said, "Avoid implementing punishments (*ḥudūd*) as much as you can, and if there is any way out for a Muslim, let him go, for it is better for a leader to make a mistake in forgiving than to make a mistake in punishing."[85]

---

[84] Q. (60:8-9).

[85] Abi Abdullah al-Hakim al-Naysaburi: *Al-Mustadrak 'ala al-Sahihayn*, Dar al-Haramayn, Cairo, 1997, vol. 4, p. 537.

HADITH 15

الحديث الخامس عشر

Islamic Morality

عَنْ أَبِي هُرَيْرَةَ ❀ أَنَّ رَسُولَ اللَّهِ (صَلَّى اللَّهُ عَلَيْهِ وَآلِهِ وَسَلَّمَ) قَالَ:
"مَنْ كَانَ يُؤْمِنُ بِاللَّهِ وَالْيَوْمِ الْآخِرِ فَلْيَقُلْ خَيْرًا أَوْ لِيَصْمُتْ، وَمَنْ كَانَ يُؤْمِنُ بِاللَّهِ
وَالْيَوْمِ الْآخِرِ فَلْيُكْرِمْ جَارَهُ، وَمَنْ كَانَ يُؤْمِنُ بِاللَّهِ وَالْيَوْمِ الْآخِرِ فَلْيُكْرِمْ ضَيْفَهُ".
رَوَاهُ الْبُخَارِيُّ وَمُسْلِمٌ.

On the authority of Abū Hurayrah (r.a.), that the Messenger of Allah (pbuh) said,

"Let him who believes in Allah and the Last Day speak good, or keep silent; and let him who believes in Allah and the Last Day be generous to his neighbor; and let him who believes in Allah and the Last Day be generous to his guest."

Related by al-Bukhārī and Muslim.

Themes

- Controlling speech
- Respecting others

Explanation

The two main themes presented in this hadith are closely related to the Islamic development of an individual.

Often, when people engage with others, they express outwardly what they harbor inside. To prevent harmful words from being spoken, a person must first cleanse their heart from ego, whims, and negative intentions. Therefore, the Prophet Muhammad (pbuh), through this hadith, indicates that if one cannot reach a level of spiritual purity to speak truthfully and maturely, then silence is often more beneficial for both the individual and others.

Uncontrolled and negative expressions lead to adverse consequences such as misinformation, insults, and lies. Imam Ghazālī, in his book Minhāj al-ʿĀbidīn, mentions a saying transmitted from the companion of the Prophet (pbuh), Abu Saʿīd al-Khuḍrī (r.a.): "When a person wakes up in the morning, his body parts address the tongue, saying: Spend the day in sincerity and worship. Avoid idle talk. If you remain straight, we will also remain straight. You go astray, we will follow you down the same path."[86]

Regarding respect towards others, the Prophet (pbuh) highlights the strong connection between faith and good conduct towards fellow humans. This once more clearly reflects Islam's high regard for sound human morality and positive values. A person with poor behavior and morals has their faith called into question.

In the hadith, there is also mention of the neighbor because they live nearby, and naturally, close relationships may develop. These relationships may often be stronger with neighbors than with relatives, as relatives might live far away, making meetings less frequent, whereas interactions with neighbors are more regular.

In some non-Muslim countries, where Muslims live among people of different faiths or those with no faith, some might not prioritize maintaining good relationships with their neighbors. This contradicts Islamic principles, which require Muslims to be courteous to everyone.

[86] Abu Hamid al-Ghazali: *Minhaj al-Abidin*, p. 339.

The Prophet Muhammad (pbuh) said in a hadith: "Gabriel kept advising me about the neighbor to the extent that I thought he would inherit (become a part of the inheritance)."[87]

Respect and care for guests also hold a special place in Islamic ethics. Believers are commanded to honor guests, especially those traveling, because travel involves hardship and fatigue. Moreover, when a person is a guest, they do not feel the same as they do in their own home. Many people around might be unfamiliar, so by respecting and caring for the guest, one ensures they do not feel uncomfortable. This religious principle regarding guests is derived from the divine treatment that Allah has accorded to humans, described in the Holy Qur'an:

"وَلَقَدْ كَرَّمْنَا بَنِي آدَمَ وَحَمَلْنَاهُمْ فِي الْبَرِّ وَالْبَحْرِ وَرَزَقْنَاهُم مِّنَ الطَّيِّبَاتِ وَفَضَّلْنَاهُمْ عَلَىٰ كَثِيرٍ مِّمَّنْ خَلَقْنَا تَفْضِيلًا"

"Indeed, We have honored the children of Adam and carried them on land and sea and provided them with good things and preferred them above many of those We created with (great) preference."[88]

[87] Muslim ibn al-Hajjaj: *Sahih Muslim*, vol. 2, p. 1214.

[88] Q. (17:70).

HADITH 16

الحديث السادس عشر

Restraining from Anger

عَنْ أَبِي هُرَيْرَةَ ﷺ أَنْ رَجُلًا قَالَ لِلنَّبِيِّ (صَلَّى اللّهُ عَلَيْهِ وَآلِهِ وَسَلَّمَ) أَوْصِنِي. قَالَ: "لَا تَغْضَبْ، فَرَدَّدَ مِرَارًا، قَالَ: لَا تَغْضَبْ".

رَوَاهُ الْبُخَارِيُّ.

On the authority of Abū Hurayrah (r.a.): A man said to the Prophet (peace and blessings of Allah be upon him), "Counsel me," so he (pbuh) said, "Do not become angry." The man repeated (his request for counsel) several times, and (each time) he (peace and blessings of Allah be upon him) said, "Do not become angry."

Related by al-Bukhārī.

Themes

- Seeking advice
- Restraint from anger

Explanation

This hadith, like the twelfth and thirteenth hadiths, is one of the four foundational hadiths that comprise Islamic morals.[89]

[89] See al-Razi: *Meshjekhah Abi Abdullah al-Razi*, p. 196

The tradition of seeking advice from wise individuals has been practiced and continues to be practiced in many places, especially in traditional Islamic environments. In these settings, it is not necessary for a person to be in difficulty to seek advice; rather, it is often done as a sign of respect towards the learned, who are farsighted and aware of the individual's circumstances. This way, they can help improve or even prevent the person from making future mistakes. Thus, the individual who approached the Prophet (pbuh) might not have been in difficulty but, out of great respect for the Messenger of Allah (pbuh) and a desire to learn something new, sought advice from him. It is possible that the Prophet (pbuh) knew that continuous anger was part of this individual's nature and advised him not to get angry to prevent future mistakes. Although the person sought to hear different advice from the Prophet (pbuh), the Messenger of Allah (pbuh) repeated the same response: "Do not get angry!"

Anger over material possession was not part of the character of the Prophet Muhammad (pbuh). He only became angry when divine teachings, which were revealed to him, were violated.[90] This does not mean that work and livelihood should be neglected; rather, true anger should be reserved for instances when the fulfillment of Islamic obligations is neglected, as this plays a significant role in a person's state in the Hereafter.

Self-control and the practice of patience are crucial in restraining anger. An event from the Prophet's (pbuh) time illustrates the importance of patience and restraint from anger. A man was verbally abusing the great companion of the Prophet (pbuh), Abu Bakr (r.a.) in the presence of the Prophet Muḥammad (pbuh). When the man saw that Abu Bakr (r.a.) was not reacting, he tried again. Abu Bakr (r.a.) still did not react but endured. When the man insulted him for the third time, Abu Bakr (r.a.) began to retaliate with words. At this moment, the Prophet (pbuh) stood up, and Abu Bakr (r.a.) asked the Prophet (pbuh), "Are you angry with me?" The Prophet (pbuh) replied, "An angel descended from the heavens who was refuting what he was saying. When you retaliated, the devil took his place. I do not sit where the devil takes place."[91]

---

90 See Muhammad ibn Isa al-Tirmidhi: *Shama'il al-Nabi*, Dar al-Gharb al-Islami, Beirut, 2000, hadith 225, p. 133.

91 Abu Dawud al-Sijistani: *Sunan Abu Dawud*, vol. 7, p. 257.

The Prophet's (pbuh) cousin and one of the members of the Prophet's (pbuh) family (*ahl al-bayt*), ʿAlī Ibn Abī Tālib (r.a), has expressed regarding anger, "The beginning of anger is madness, and its end is regret."[92]

The devil is the one who incites a person to anger. For this reason, the Qur'an and prophetic guidance contain instructions to protect a person from the whispers of the accursed devil. The Qur'an says,

"وَإِمَّا يَنزَغَنَّكَ مِنَ الشَّيْطَانِ نَزْغٌ فَاسْتَعِذْ بِاللَّهِ إِنَّهُ هُوَ السَّمِيعُ الْعَلِيمُ"

"And if an evil whisper comes to you from Satan, then seek refuge in Allah. Verily, He is All-Hearer, All-Knower."[93]

During a time of anger, the Prophet (pbuh) has instructed believers to seek Allah's protection against the devil. He also mentioned that in moments of anger, one should sit if they are standing or lay down if anger doesn't go away.[94]

The Prophet's advice to seek Allah's protection and to change physical positions (sitting or lying down) can be likened to modern recommendations for taking a "timeout." This practice allows individuals to step back from the situation and regain control over their emotions, similar to the advice from various psychology experts who suggest taking short breaks during stressful moments.[95]

---

[92] Muhammad ibn Muflih al-Maqdisi: *Al-Adab al-Shar'iyyah*, Mu'assasat al-Risalah, 3rd edition, Beirut, 1999, vol. 1, p. 205.

[93] Q. (41:36).

[94] Abu Dawud al-Sijistani: *Sunan Abi Dawud*, vol. 7, p. 162.

[95] Tchiki Davis, "Managing Anger: Tips, Techniques, and Tools," *Psychology Today*, accessed October 12, 2024, https://www.psychologytoday.com/us/blog/click-here-happiness/202203/managing-anger-tips-techniques-and-tools.

HADITH 17

الحديث السابع عشر

Manifesting Benevolence (Iḥsān)

عَنْ أَبِي يَعْلَى شَدَّادِ بْنِ أَوْسٍ ﷺ عَنْ رَسُولِ اللَّهِ (صَلَّى اللّهُ عَلَيْهِ وَآلِهِ وَسَلَّمَ) قَالَ: "إِنَّ اللَّهَ كَتَبَ الْإِحْسَانَ عَلَى كُلِّ شَيْءٍ، فَإِذَا قَتَلْتُمْ فَأَحْسِنُوا الْقِتْلَةَ، وَإِذَا ذَبَحْتُمْ فَأَحْسِنُوا الذِّبْحَةَ، وَلْيُحِدَّ أَحَدُكُمْ شَفْرَتَهُ، وَلْيُرِحْ ذَبِيحَتَهُ".

رَوَاهُ مُسْلِمٌ.

On the authority of Abū Ya'lā Shaddād bin Aws (r.a.), that the Messenger of Allah (pbuh) said,

"Verily Allah has prescribed kindness in all things. So if you kill then kill well; and if you slaughter, then slaughter well. Let each one of you sharpen his blade and let him spare suffering to the animal he slaughters."

Related by Muslim.

Theme

- The vital role of kindness in every act, no matter how small

Explanation

The beginning of this hadith calls for the demonstration of kindness in everything and it highlights the positive and unique role of Islam in human life. It also affirms the universality of its message, focusing not only on the fulfillment of religious rituals but also on the exhibition of kindness in every action.

Kindness is emphasized even in the act of slaughtering an animal, reminding humans that they are dealing with Allah's creatures, no matter how insignificant the animal may seem. By highlighting the importance of showing kindness during slaughter, the hadith encourages deeper reflection on the greater rewards associated with demonstrating kindness in all actions, particularly those of greater significance. To illustrate this hadith with an example, we can refer to a saying of the Messenger of Allah (pbuh) about the importance and reward for someone who provides a fasting person with something as simple as water or milk to break their fast: "Whoever provides *iftar* to a fasting person will have their sins forgiven and be saved from punishment. They will also receive the same reward as the fasting person without diminishing the fasting person's reward in the least." People said, "Not all of us can afford to give *iftar* to a fasting person." The Prophet replied: "Allah grants this reward to anyone who gives a fasting person a single date, a sip of water, or a mixture of milk and water."[96]

This raises the question: If such a great reward is given to someone who performs the simple act of offering water to a fasting person, how much greater might the reward be for someone who helps another human being out of suffering and misery?

Another crucial point derived from the hadith is that while Allah has permitted the consumption of certain types of animals, this does not justify killing them for consumption in a brutal manner, using methods that cause prolonged suffering until their last breath or causing them to die without proper slaughter. Unfortunately, such inhumane practices occur in many places, driven by the meat industry's hasty ambitions to reduce time and increase profits.

---

96 Muhammed Ibn Khuzaymah: *Sahih ibn Khuzaymah*, Al-Maktab Al-Islami, Beirut, 1970, vol. 3, p. 191.

HADITH 18

الحديث الثامن عشر

Following a Bad Deed with a Good One

عَنْ أَبِي ذَرٍّ جُنْدَبِ بْنِ جُنَادَةَ، وَأَبِي عَبْدِ الرَّحْمَنِ مُعَاذِ بْنِ جَبَلٍ رَضِيَ اللَّهُ عَنْهُمَا، عَنْ رَسُولِ اللَّهِ (صَلَّى اللَّهُ عَلَيْهِ وَآلِهِ وَسَلَّمَ) قَالَ:
"اتَّقِ اللَّهَ حَيْثُمَا كُنْت، وَأَتْبِعْ السَّيِّئَةَ الْحَسَنَةَ تَمْحُهَا، وَخَالِقْ النَّاسَ بِخُلُقٍ حَسَنٍ".
رَوَاهُ التِّرْمِذِيُّ وَقَالَ: حَدِيثٌ حَسَنٌ، وَفِي بَعْضِ النُّسَخِ: حَسَنٌ صَحِيحٌ.

On the authority of Abū Dharr Jundub ibn Junādah, and Abū ʿAbdur-Raḥmān Mucadh bin Jabal (r.a.), that the Messenger of Allah (pbuh) said,

"Have fear of Allah (*taqwā*) wherever you may be, and follow up a bad deed with a good deed which will wipe it out, and behave well towards the people."

It was related by al-Tirmidhī, who said it was a sound (*ḥasan*) hadith, and in some scripts, it is stated to be a reliable-authentic (*ḥasan saḥiḥ*) hadith.

Themes

- Fear of Allah (*taqwā*)
- Replacing a bad deed with a good one
- Kindness towards people

Explanation

The term *taqwā* is mentioned in numerous verses of the Qur'an, urging believers to strive for it. This word, referenced in the hadith, is often translated as devotion, dedication, mindfulness, or fear of Allah. The notable scholar, Muhammad al-Shāmī (d. 942/1535), in his book, *Subul al-Hudā wa al-Rashād*, provides a linguistic definition: "expressing oneself with few words."[97] The lexicographer Ibn Fāris (d. 395/1004) defines *taqwā* as fear and caution, rooted in fearing worshiping any deity other than Allah (*shirk*), avoiding sins, and abstaining from dubious or corrupt actions.[98] Regarding the essence of *taqwā*, it entails submission to Allah rather than defiance. ʿAli (r.a.), when asked about *taqwā*, replied:

"اَلتَّقْوَى هِيَ الْخَوْفُ مِنَ الْجَلِيلِ وَالْعَمَلُ بِالتَّنْزِيلِ وَالْقَنَاعَةُ بِالْقَلِيلِ وَالِاسْتِعْدَادُ لِيَوْمِ الرَّحِيلِ"

"*Taqwā* means: Fear of the Almighty, acting according to Divine Revelation (the Qur'an), contentment with little, and readiness for the Day of Departure."[99]

Taqwā forms the cornerstone of many Islamic acts of worship. By fearing Allah in all aspects of life, as highlighted in this hadith, one becomes more conscientious about their deeds, thereby avoiding sin. Beyond its preventative role, it strengthens the bond with Allah, fostering a deeper remembrance of Him. Those who fear Allah in all situations are less likely to engage in hypocrisy or harm Allah's creation, as they are sensitive to His Divine Presence. In contrast, the irreligious may fear the law or individuals and act inconsistently when not under scrutiny.

The hadith also underscores the importance of replacing bad deeds with good ones, as this eradicates the former. Such emphasis reflects

---

[97] Muhammad al-Shami: *Subul al-Huda wa al-Rashad*, Dar al-Kutb al-Ilmiyyah, Beirut, 1993, vol. 1, p. 421.

[98] Ibid.

[99] Ibid.

Allah's profound desire to forgive believers' mistakes and His aspiration for their continuous improvement.

Lastly, the hadith stresses the application of noble morals. Allah has adorned human behavior with the display of good morals. The Messenger of Allah (pbuh) possessed the best morals of all people, as described in the Qur'an:

"وَإِنَّكَ لَعَلَى خُلُقٍ عَظِيمٍ"

"You (O Muhammad) are truly of a great moral character."[100]

In the book, Al-Adab al-Mufrad by Muḥammad ibn Isma'īl al-Bukhārī, which compiles hadiths related to morality, the Prophet (pbuh) himself stated the purpose of his mission: "Verily, I have been sent to perfect the best moral character."[101]

Good morals, like intellect, are a gift from Allah to humanity, setting them apart from other creatures. Through sincere adherence to good conduct and obedience to Allah, societies can uphold high values, facilitate effective communication, and foster peace, harmony, and developmental opportunities among people.

Demonstrating good conduct not only reflects love for the Prophet of Allah (pbuh) but also strengthens the spiritual connection between individuals and their Creator, paving the way for entry into Paradise. Prophet Muhammad (pbuh) once asked his companions who among them would be dearest and closest to him on the Day of Judgment. They asked him to tell them, to which he replied, "Those with the best manners."[102]

---

[100] Q. (68:4).

[101] Muhammad Ibn Ismail al-Bukhari: *Book of Muslim's Moral and Manners*, translated from Arabic to English by Yusuf Talal deLorenzo, USA Al-Saadawi Publications, Alexandria, USA, 1999, p. 126.

[102] Ibid. p. 125.

HADITH 19

الحديث التاسع عشر

Relationships with the Creator

عَنْ عَبْدِ اللَّهِ بْنِ عَبَّاسٍ رَضِيَ اللَّهُ عَنْهُمَا قَالَ: كُنْت خَلْفَ رَسُولِ اللَّهِ (صَلَّى اللَّهُ عَلَيْهِ وَآلِهِ وَسَلَّمَ) يَوْمًا، فَقَالَ:

"يَا غُلَامِ! إنِّي أُعَلِّمُك كَلِمَاتٍ: احْفَظْ اللَّهَ يَحْفَظْك، احْفَظْ اللَّهَ تَجِدْهُ تُجَاهَك، إذَا سَأَلْت فَاسْأَلْ اللَّه وَإِذَا اسْتَعَنْت فَاسْتَعِنْ بِاَللَّهِ، وَاعْلَمْ أَنَّ الْأُمَّةَ لَوْ اجْتَمَعَتْ عَلَى أَنْ يَنْفَعُوك بِشَيْءٍ لَمْ يَنْفَعُوك إلَّا بِشَيْءٍ قَدْ كَتَبَهُ اللَّهُ لَك، وَإِنْ اجْتَمَعُوا عَلَى أَنْ يَضُرُّوك بِشَيْءٍ لَمْ يَضُرُّوك إلَّا بِشَيْءٍ قَدْ كَتَبَهُ اللَّهُ عَلَيْك؛ رُفِعَتْ الْأَقْلَامُ، وَجَفَّتْ الصُّحُفُ".

رَوَاهُ التِّرْمِذِيُّ وَقَالَ: حَدِيثٌ حَسَنٌ صَحِيحٌ. وَفِي رِوَايَةِ غَيْرِ التِّرْمِذِيِّ: "احْفَظْ اللَّهَ تَجِدْهُ أمامك، تَعَرَّفْ إلَى اللَّهِ فِي الرَّخَاءِ يَعْرِفُك فِي الشِّدَّةِ، وَاعْلَمْ أَنَّ مَا أَخْطَأَك لَمْ يَكُنْ لِيُصِيبَك، وَمَا أَصَابَك لَمْ يَكُنْ لِيُخْطِئَك، وَاعْلَمْ أَنَّ النَّصْرَ مَعَ الصَّبْرِ، وَأَنْ الْفَرَجَ مَعَ الْكَرْبِ، وَأَنَّ مَعَ الْعُسْرِ يُسْرًا".

On the authority of ʿAbdullāh Ibn ʿAbbās (r.a.) who said: One day I was behind the Prophet (pbuh) (riding on the same mount) and he said,

"O young man, I shall teach you some words (of advice): Be mindful of Allah and Allah will protect you. Be mindful of Allah and you will find Him in front of you. If you ask, then ask Allah (alone); and if you seek help, then seek help from Allah (alone). And know that if the nation were to gather together to benefit you with anything, they would not benefit you except with what Allah had already prescribed for you. And if they were to gather together to harm you with anything, they would not harm you except with what Allah had already prescribed against you. The pens have been lifted and the pages have dried."

It was related by al-Tirmidhī, who said it was a reliable-authentic hadith. Another narration, other than that of al-Tirmidhī, reads: "Be mindful of Allah, and you will find Him in front of you. Recognize and acknowledge Allah in times of ease and prosperity, and He will remember you in times of adversity. And know that what has passed you by (and you have failed to attain) was not going to befall you, and what has befallen you was not going to pass you by. And know that victory comes with patience, relief with affliction, and hardship with ease."

Theme

- Building a sound relationship with the Creator

Explanation

Through this hadith, the Prophet (pbuh) instructs the young man, Ibn ʿAbbās, on establishing a proper relationship with his Creator through two primary avenues: firstly, through care, prayer, and seeking assistance from Allah; secondly, by believing in Allah's decrees.

It is essential to highlight that the Prophet (pbuh) consistently engaged in dialogue and provided guidance to young people whenever possible. In the initial guidance, the Messenger of Allah's statement, "Be mindful of Allah, and He will take care of you," signifies not that God requires humans to care for Him, but rather emphasizes the importance for humans to be attentive to Divine teachings and live accordingly. By doing so, Allah will indeed bestow His special favors upon them.

Furthermore, it is mentioned, "Be mindful of Allah, and you will find Him in front of you." This does not imply that Allah will manifest physically before humans, but rather denotes that His mercy, assistance, and support will be with those who believe and act in accordance with the Qur'an and the traditions of the Prophet (pbuh).

The hadith also emphasizes prayer and reliance on Allah. These two qualities foster a profound bond between Allah and humanity. Prayer and reliance on Allah are not merely verbal expressions; they originate from sincere devotion. They should be practiced not only in times of hardship but in all situations. Prayer infused with heartfelt sincerity in various circumstances strengthens the intimate relationship between Allah and humanity. It is for this reason that Allah encourages in His Noble Qur'an,

"وَقَالَ رَبُّكُمُ ادْعُونِي أَسْتَجِبْ لَكُمْ"

"And your Lord says, 'Call upon Me; I will respond to you.'"[103]

In numerous Qur'anic verses, humans are encouraged to take the initiative towards Allah, so that Allah may respond to them. For instance, in another verse, it is illustrated how Allah guides a person correctly when they respond to Him and have faith in Him,

"فَلْيَسْتَجِيبُوا لِي وَلْيُؤْمِنُوا بِي لَعَلَّهُمْ يَرْشُدُونَ"

"So let them respond to Me and believe in Me that they may be guided."[104]

Furthermore, in this hadith, the Messenger of Allah emphasizes the importance of believing in Allah's decree (*qadar*), which is one of the six pillars of Islamic belief. By accepting Allah's decree and acknowledging that everything originates from Him, humans strengthen their trust and connection with their Creator. Believing that everything that happens was meant to happen and that whatever will come is ultimately beneficial for believers, empowers them to confront challenges in this world and stand resolute against falsehood and injustice. Thus, belief in Allah's decree transforms humans from fearing the creations of the Creator to fearing the Creator of creations, empowering them to succeed in life as Allah's

---

[103] Q. (40:60).

[104] Q. (2:186).

support is ever-present. This is confirmed in the Qur'anic verse where Allah declares,

"إِنَّ اللَّهَ يُدَافِعُ عَنِ الَّذِينَ آمَنُوا"

"Indeed, Allah defends those who have believed."[105]

[105] Q. (22:38).

HADITH 20

الحديث العشرون

Modesty: A Prophetic Counsel

عَنْ ابْنِ مَسْعُودٍ عُقْبَةَ بْنِ عَمْرٍو الْأَنْصَارِيِّ الْبَدْرِيِّ ﷺ قَالَ: قَالَ رَسُولُ اللَّهِ (صَلَّى اللَّهُ عَلَيْهِ وَآلِهِ وَسَلَّمَ):
"إِنَّ مِمَّا أَدْرَكَ النَّاسُ مِنْ كَلَامِ النُّبُوَّةِ الْأُولَى: إِذَا لَمْ تَسْتَحِ فَاصْنَعْ مَا شِئْتَ".
رَوَاهُ الْبُخَارِيُّ.

On the authority of Abū Masʿūd cUqbah bin ʿAmr al-Anṣārī al-Badrī (r.a.) who said: The Messenger of Allah (pbuh) said,

"Verily, from what was learned by the people from the speech of the earliest prophecy is: If you feel no shame, then do as you wish."

Related by al-Bukhārī.

Themes

- The significance of embodying modesty, as conveyed through the unified Divine Teachings of God's Messengers
- The relationship between Islam and other Abrahamic faiths, emphasizing that Islam is not a new doctrine but a continuation of the Divine teachings

Explanation

In this hadith, the term *ḥayāʾ* is mentioned, commonly translated as "modesty." However, this word encompasses additional meanings, including "sensitivity."

The esteemed Muslim scholar Dhū al-Nūn al-Miṣrī (d. 244-859) described *ḥayāʾ* as a profound feeling within the heart, characterized by the fear of God due to past mistakes.[106]

The expression in this hadith, "If you have no shame, do as you wish," should not be taken literally. It indicates that a lack of modesty can lead a person to commit any prohibited act without regard for religious and social norms. It's akin to a parent telling their child, "If you don't follow my advice, then do as you wish." This does not imply that the parent is giving the child the freedom to choose any option, including bad ones, but rather expressing their frustration and dissatisfaction if the advice is ignored. Therefore, the Prophet (pbuh) in this hadith emphasizes the importance of maintaining modesty. Without it, a person opens the door to sinful actions and becomes accustomed to committing them, eventually reaching a point where they feel devoid of modesty and free to commit sins. Such an attitude also incurs God's displeasure.

Modesty is closely linked with faith. The Messenger of Allah (pbuh) states in a hadith,

"الإِيمَانُ عُرْيَانٌ وَلِبَاسُهُ التَّقْوَى وزينته الحياء وَمَالُهُ الْعِفَّةُ"

"Faith (*al-īmān*) is bare. Its garment is piety, its adornment is modesty, and its wealth is chastity (*al-ʿiffah*)."[107]

It is crucial to understand the phrase in this hadith which highlights that modesty is among the earliest prophetic teachings. This proves that Islam did not begin 1400 years ago but has been present since the time of the first human and prophet, Adam (pbuh). Islam did not come to

---

106 Abu al-Qasim al-Qushayri: *Al-Risalah al-Qushayriyyah*, Matbaʾ Muʾassasat Dar al-Shaʾb, Cairo, 1989, p. 372.

107 Ibn Abi al-Dunya: *Makarim al-Akhlaq*, Maktabah al-Quran, Cairo, 1990, p. 41.

abolish the divine messages of other heavenly faiths but to correct and reinforce the messages that had been altered over time. This was done under the guidance of the Seal of the Prophets, Muhammad (pbuh). Therefore, those who embrace and follow his guidance are truly adhering to the righteous path that God has revealed to humanity through His messengers throughout history. In the Qur'an it states,

"وَأَنْزَلْنَا إِلَيْكَ الْكِتَابَ بِالْحَقِّ مُصَدِّقًا لِمَا بَيْنَ يَدَيْهِ مِنَ الْكِتَابِ وَمُهَيْمِنًا عَلَيْهِ فَاحْكُمْ بَيْنَهُمْ بِمَا أَنْزَلَ اللَّهُ وَلَا تَتَّبِعْ أَهْوَاءَهُمْ عَمَّا جَاءَكَ مِنَ الْحَقِّ لِكُلٍّ جَعَلْنَا مِنْكُمْ شِرْعَةً وَمِنْهَاجًا وَلَوْ شَاءَ اللَّهُ لَجَعَلَكُمْ أُمَّةً وَاحِدَةً وَلَكِنْ لِيَبْلُوَكُمْ فِي مَا آتَاكُمْ فَاسْتَبِقُوا الْخَيْرَاتِ إِلَى اللَّهِ مَرْجِعُكُمْ جَمِيعًا فَيُنَبِّئُكُمْ بِمَا كُنْتُمْ فِيهِ تَخْتَلِفُونَ"

"And We have revealed to you, (O Muhammad), the Book in truth, confirming that which preceded it of the Scripture and as a criterion over it. So judge between them by what Allah has revealed and do not follow their inclinations away from what has come to you of the truth. To each of you We prescribed a law and a method. Had Allah willed, He would have made you one nation (united in religion), but (He intended) to test you in what He has given you; so race to (all that is) good. To Allah is your return all together, and He will (then) inform you concerning that over which you used to differ."[108]

People may exhibit modesty before others or even in their personal conduct, yet true modesty before God surpasses these superficial forms. The Prophet (pbuh) exemplified true modesty before Allah in a hadith narrated by Ibn Masʿūd (r.a.): "He once addressed his companions, saying, 'Have modesty before Allah as it is rightfully due!' They responded, 'We are indeed modest, O Messenger of Allah.' He clarified, 'That is not what I mean. True modesty before Allah entails safeguarding one's thoughts and intentions, managing what one consumes, and contemplating the inevitability of death and its trials. Whoever seeks the Hereafter should forsake the fleeting pleasures of this world. Those who adhere to these

[108] Q. (5:48).

principles have indeed achieved true modesty before Allah as it should be.'"[109]

People of profound spiritual sensitivity, beyond the mentioned practices, feel modest before Allah when it comes to relying on, fearing, and finding hope in His creations. They place their reliance, fear, and hope solely in Him, viewing His creations as conveyors of His decree rather than arbiters of destiny. As an illustration of this, "It is recounted that some individuals once passed by a person sleeping in a dense forest with a horse nearby. They asked, 'Aren't you afraid to sleep in such a terrifying place among wild animals?' The man lifted his head and replied, 'I feel ashamed before God to fear anyone other than Him.' He then lowered his head and resumed his sleep."[110]

---

[109] Ebu al-Kasim al-Qushayri: *Al-Risalah al-Qushayriyyah,* p. 372.

[110] Ibid. p. 374.

HADITH 21

الحديث الحادي والعشرون

Steadfastness in Faith

عَنْ أَبِي عَمْرٍو وَقِيلَ: أَبِي عَمْرَةَ سُفْيَانَ بْنِ عَبْدِ اللَّهِ قَالَ:
"قُلْتُ: يَا رَسُولَ اللَّهِ! قُلْ لِي فِي الْإِسْلَامِ قَوْلًا لَا أَسْأَلُ عَنْهُ أَحَدًا غَيْرَكَ؛ قَالَ: قُلْ: آمَنْتُ بِاَللَّهِ ثُمَّ اسْتَقِمْ".
رَوَاهُ مُسْلِمٌ.

On the authority of Abū ʿAmr — and he is also called Abū ʿAmrah Sufyān bin ʿAbdullāh al- Thaqafī (r.a.) who said,

"I said, 'O Messenger of Allah, tell me something about Islam which I can ask of no one but you.' He (pbuh) said, 'Say: I believe in Allah — and then be steadfast.'"

Related by Muslim.

Theme

- The importance of steadfastness in Islam (*al-Istiqāmah*)

Explanation

This hadith illustrates the prophetic wisdom of Prophet Muhammad (pbuh), guiding Muslims on how to truly embody their faith by believing and remaining steadfast in actions that confirm their beliefs. According to the famous Muslim scholar, Abū Al-Qāsim Al-Qushayrī (d. 465/1072), steadfastness in faith, known as "*istiqāmah*," entails unwavering adherence to the principles of faith without compromise. Those who embody the essence of steadfastness in Islam, which is centered on the Oneness of Allah (*tawḥīd*), are shielded from the eternal consequences of Hellfire. Furthermore, perfecting steadfastness in faith provides protection from trials without being swayed by calamities."[111]

Being steadfast in Islam is challenging because it requires a constant struggle against desires, the devil, and adversarial individuals. Even the Messenger of Allah (pbuh) faced difficulties in achieving steadfastness. When asked about the reason for the grayness of his hair, he replied: "My hair has turned gray because of Surah Hūd and its companions (other surahs)."[112] Surah Hūd contains a Qur'anic verse advising the Messenger of Allah and the believers to remain firm and unwavering in Islam,

"فَاسْتَقِمْ كَمَا أُمِرْتَ وَمَن تَابَ مَعَكَ"

"So remain steadfast as you have been commanded, along with those who have turned back (repent) with you."[113]

This hadith further illustrates the reverence of the believers towards the Messenger of Allah (pbuh). Their respect is evident in their eagerness to seek life guidance directly from him, without needing to consult anyone else.

Alongside emphasizing devotion in worship, there is also an imperative for the believer to direct their heart towards Allah. Just as the mind is focused on performing rituals completely and punctually, the heart should similarly be dedicated to purging all that is transient and connecting with the Eternal One, Allah.

---

111 Abu al-Qasim al-Qushayri: *Al-Risalah al-Qushayriyyah*, p. 356.

112 Abi Ya'la al-Musali: *Musnad Abi Ya'la al-Musali*, Dar al-Ma'mun lil-Turath, 1989, Damascus, volume 2, p. 184.

113 Q. (11:112).

HADITH 22

الحديث الثاني والعشرون

The Simplicity of Islam

عَنْ أَبِي عَبْدِ اللَّهِ جَابِرِ بْنِ عَبْدِ اللَّهِ الْأَنْصَارِيِّ رَضِيَ اللَّهُ عَنْهُمَا:
"أَنَّ رَجُلًا سَأَلَ رَسُولَ اللَّهِ (صَلَّى اللَّهُ عَلَيْهِ وَآلِهِ وَسَلَّمَ) فَقَالَ: أَرَأَيْت إذَا صَلَّيْت الْمَكْتُوبَاتِ، وَصُمْت رَمَضَانَ، وَأَحْلَلْت الْحَلَالَ، وَحَرَّمْت الْحَرَامَ، وَلَمْ أَزِدْ عَلَى ذَلِكَ شَيْئًا؛ أَأَدْخُلُ الْجَنَّةَ؟ قَالَ: نَعَمْ".
رَوَاهُ مُسْلِمٌ.

On the authority of Abū ʿAbdull-llāh Jābir bin ʿAbdil-lāh al-Anṣāri (r.a.) that: A man questioned the Messenger of Allah (peace and blessings of Allah be upon him) and said, "Do you think that if I perform the obligatory prayers, fast in Ramadan, treat as lawful that which is halal, and treat as forbidden that which is haram, and do not increase upon that (in voluntary good deeds), then I shall enter Paradise?" He (pbuh) replied, "Yes."

Related by Muslim.

Theme

- Simplicity in Islamic practice and attaining entry into Paradise

Explanation

In this hadith, the Messenger of Allah illustrates the simplicity of Islamic practice. The hadith also emphasizes adhering to what is permissible and abstaining from what is forbidden. This encompasses not only avoiding alcohol and pork but also distancing oneself from negative traits such as selfishness, lying, backbiting, jealousy, and arrogance. Furthermore, adhering to what is permissible involves not only dietary restrictions like food, drink, work, and sleep but also encompasses good conduct, frequent remembrance of Allah, and serving those in need.

A question arises: Why does this hadith mention only certain conditions of Islam and not others? Some scholars suggest that at the time of the query to the Messenger of Allah (pbuh), obligations like *zakat* and *hajj* were not obligatory, and the Declaration of Islamic Faith (*shahādah*) is inherently understood by the questioner as a Muslim believer. Therefore, explicit mention of these aspects was unnecessary in that context.

HADITH 23

الحديث الثالث والعشرون

Defining Islamic Rituals

عَنْ أَبِي مَالِكٍ الْحَارِثِ بْنِ عَاصِمٍ الْأَشْعَرِيِّ قَالَ: قَالَ رَسُولُ اللَّهِ (صَلَّى اللَّهُ عَلَيْهِ وَآلِهِ وَسَلَّمَ):

"الطُّهُورُ شَطْرُ الْإِيمَانِ، وَالْحَمْدُ لِلَّهِ تَمْلَأُ الْمِيزَانَ، وَسُبْحَانَ اللَّهِ وَالْحَمْدُ لِلَّهِ تَمْلَآنِ -أَوْ: تَمْلَأُ- مَا بَيْنَ السَّمَاءِ وَالْأَرْضِ، وَالصَّلَاةُ نُورٌ، وَالصَّدَقَةُ بُرْهَانٌ، وَالصَّبْرُ ضِيَاءٌ، وَالْقُرْآنُ حُجَّةٌ لَكَ أَوْ عَلَيْكَ، كُلُّ النَّاسِ يَغْدُو، فَبَائِعٌ نَفْسَهُ فَمُعْتِقُهَا أَوْ مُوبِقُهَا".

رَوَاهُ مُسْلِمٌ.

On the authority of Abū Mālik al-Ḥārith ibn ʿĀṣim al-Ashʿarī (r.a.) who said: The Messenger of Allah (pbuh) said,

"Purity is half of faith (īman). Al-ḥamdu lil-lāh (praise be to Allah) fills the scales, and *subḥān-Allah* (how far from imperfection is Allah) and *al-ḥamdu lil-lāh* fill that which is between heaven and earth. And the prayer (*ṣalāh*) is a light, and charity is a proof, and patience is illumination, and the Qur'an is a proof either for you or against you. Every person starts his day as a vendor of his soul, either freeing it or bringing about its ruin."

Related by Muslim.

Theme

- Emphasizing the importance of purity, remembrance of Allah (*dhikr*), Prayer (*salāh*), Charity (*sadaqah*), Patience (*sabr*), the Qur'an, distinguishing good deeds from evil ones, and practicing righteous acts.

Explanation

From the outset of this hadith, the Messenger of Allah (pbuh) emphasizes the importance of purity, illustrating that physical purity is a reflection of spiritual purity. What value would physical cleanliness hold if it did not influence spiritual cleanliness at all? It's like a house that appears clean on the outside but is filthy inside, emitting a foul odor. While the external appearance of a house matters, its true beauty, tranquility, and purity lie within, as one lives inside its walls. Therefore, for sincere believers, physical purity symbolizes spiritual cleanliness. Physical purity is achieved through washing the entire body or specific parts of it, while spiritual purity begins with repentance (*tawbah*) before the Almighty.

Some scholars have noted that in the first sentence of this hadith, the focus is not on faith itself but on prayer (*salāh*), which during the Prophet's (pbuh) time was often associated with the word "faith" (*īmān*). Thus, bodily cleanliness for performing religious rituals, including ablution, *ghusl*, and *tayammum*, is a prerequisite for prayer, being considered as half of the prayer itself.[114]

Furthermore, the Messenger of Allah (pbuh) emphasizes that praising and showing gratitude to God (*al-ḥamd*) carries significant weight on the scale of good deeds (*al-mīzān*). On the Day of Judgment, people's deeds will be weighed, and those with more good deeds will enter Paradise. These deeds gain even more value when the phrase *al-ḥamdu li-lāh* is mentioned frequently. Scholars have noted that to properly exalt and praise Allah, one must avoid being untrustworthy or ungrateful towards Him.[115]

---

[114] See Zain al-Din ibn Shihab al-Din: *Jami' al-Ulum wa al-Hikam*, Dar Ibn Kathir, Damascus, 2008, p. 492.

[115] See Abu Hamid al-Ghazali: *Minhaj al-Abidin*, p.319.

In his book *Al-Risālah al-Qushayriyyah*, Imam Al-Qushayrī explains that gratitude to Allah is expressed not only through words but also through the actions of the body and the heart. Thanking Allah with the limbs means that a person should embody loyalty to Allah and serve Him with their entire being. This involves ensuring that the mouth, hands, eyes, and other parts of the body adhere to divine teachings by avoiding the forbidden and fulfilling religious obligations. Thanking Allah with the heart means that the believer should detach from material concerns and focus on the Unity of Allah (*tawḥīd*), consistently showing respect to Him in every moment and situation.[116]

In the hadith under discussion, the Prophet Muhammad (pbuh) highlights the immense value of the phrase "praise and thanks belong to Allah" (*subḥān Allāh wa al- ḥamdu li-llāh*). He emphasizes that if this phrase were to take physical form, it would fill the entire space between heaven and earth.

Expressions such as "*subḥān Allāh wa al- ḥamdu li-llāh*" are utterances that connect one with their Creator. These acts of remembrance soothe the soul, increase awareness of Allah's presence, and earn His approval. The continuous practice of mentioning and remembering Allah through such phrases is emphasized in several Qur'anic verses and Prophetic sayings. In the Qur'an, it is said,

"يَا أَيُّهَا الَّذِينَ آمَنُوا اذْكُرُوا اللَّهَ ذِكْرًا كَثِيرًا وَسَبِّحُوهُ بُكْرَةً وَأَصِيلًا"

"O you who have believed, remember Allah with much remembrance and exalt Him morning and afternoon."[117]

By frequently invoking these expressions, believers draw closer to Allah and cultivate a deeper sense of spirituality and gratitude.

Furthermore, the Messenger of Allah explains that prayer (*salāh*) is light. It is called light because it protects the believers from sin, guiding

---

[116] See Abu al-Qasim al-Qushayri: *Al-Risalah al-Qushayriyyah*, p. 312.

[117] Q. (33:41).

them through the darkness of wrongdoing.[118] In the Qur'an, it is said,

"اتْلُ مَا أُوحِيَ إِلَيْكَ مِنَ الْكِتَابِ وَأَقِمِ الصَّلَاةَ إِنَّ الصَّلَاةَ تَنْهَىٰ عَنِ الْفَحْشَاءِ وَالْمُنكَرِ وَلَذِكْرُ اللَّهِ أَكْبَرُ وَاللَّهُ يَعْلَمُ مَا تَصْنَعُونَ"

"Recite what has been revealed to you of the Book and establish prayer. Indeed, prayer prohibits immorality and wrongdoing, and the remembrance of Allah is greater. And Allah knows what you do."[119]

As for charity (*ṣadaqah*), the Messenger of Allah (pbuh) refers to it as a proof (*burhān*) of one's sincere and sound faith, which will testify on their behalf on the Day of Judgment.

Additionally, Prophet Muhammad (pbuh) describes patience (*ṣabr*) as a radiant light (*ḍiyāʾ*), likening it to the sun's light, which not only illuminates but also provides warmth. This contrasts with the moon's light (*nūr*), which merely reflects the sun's radiance without producing warmth. Allah clarifies this distinction in the Qur'an:

"هُوَ الَّذِي جَعَلَ الشَّمْسَ ضِيَاءً وَالْقَمَرَ نُورًا"

"It is He who made the sun a shining light and the moon a derived light."[120]

Through these metaphors, the Prophet (pbuh) highlights the transformative power of prayer, charity, and patience in a believer's life.

In the book *Sharḥ al-Taftāzānī* by Imam Saʿad al-Dīn Masʿūd Taftāzānī, it is mentioned that patience (*ṣabr*) holds even greater value than prayer (*salāh*), which is described as light (*nūr*) in this hadith. The Imam argues that patience is foundational, as it underpins the pillars of faith and Islamic practice, thereby elevating it above prayer.[121]

---

118 See the explanation of Sa'd al-Din Masud bin Umar bin Abd Allah: *Sharh al-Taftazani ala al-Arbain al-Nawawiyyah*, p. 146.

119 Q (29:45).

120 Q. (10:5).

121 See the explanation of Sa'd al-Din Masud bin Umar bin Abd Allah: *Sharh al-Taftazani ala al-Arbain al-Nawawiyyah*, pg 147.

Also, Imam Ghazālī, in his book *Minhāj al-'Ābidīn*, describes patience as a bitter and unpleasant remedy, yet one with numerous virtues. He states, "Patience is a very bitter and unpleasant remedy, but it has so many virtues that through it you can easily achieve victories and avoid all harms and injuries. Wise people dare to take the bitter dose, without worrying about the taste, thinking that enduring the bitter moment ensures victories in the years to come."[122] This sentiment is echoed in the Qur'an:

"مَا عِندَكُمْ يَنفَدُ وَمَا عِندَ اللَّهِ بَاقٍ وَلَنَجْزِيَنَّ الَّذِينَ صَبَرُوا أَجْرَهُم بِأَحْسَنِ مَا كَانُوا يَعْمَلُونَ"

"Whatever you have will end, but what Allah has is lasting. And We will surely give those who were patient their reward according to the best of what they used to do."[123]

Through patience, believers can achieve great victories and avoid harm, earning the lasting rewards that Allah has promised.

Furthermore, Imam Ghazālī identifies four categories of patience:

1. Patience in obedience to Allah (*ṣabr ʿalā al-ṭāʿah*): This involves steadfastness in performing acts of worship and fulfilling religious obligations.

2. Patience in abstaining from sins (ṣabr ʿalā al-maʿṣiyah): This entails resisting temptations and refraining from sinful behavior.

3. Patience in facing worldly trials (ṣabr ʿalā maṣāʾib al-dunyā): This refers to enduring hardships and adversities with resilience and faith.

4. Patience in avoiding excessive and unnecessary worldly matters (ṣabr ʿalā fuḍūl al-dunyā): This involves maintaining self-control and not overindulging in material pursuits.[124]

In the aforementioned hadith, the Messenger of Allah (pbuh) states that the Qur'an is a proof either for or against a person. This means

---

[122] Abu Hamid al-Ghazali: *Minhaj al-Abidin*, p. 238.

[123] Q. (16:96).

[124] Abu Hamid Gazali: *Minhaj al-Abidin*, p. 238.

that if a believer adheres to the Qur'an's guidance and acts upon it, the Qur'an will testify and intercede on their behalf before Allah on the Day of Judgment. Conversely, if someone neglects its guidance and fails to act accordingly, the Qur'an will testify against them.

In the final part of this hadith, Prophet Muhammad (pbuh) says that each person begins their day as a trader of their soul. They may either free or destroy it. This expression is used figuratively to illustrate that from morning till evening, a person either succumbs to their desires and the cursed devil by committing sins, or lives in submission to Allah, following the guidance of faith. Those who submit to their desires or the devil become their servants and ultimately destroy themselves, while those who submit to Allah become His servants and achieve salvation.

HADITH 24

الحديث الرابع والعشرون

The Infinity of Divine Blessings

عَنْ أَبِي ذَرٍّ الْغِفَارِيِّ عَنْ النَّبِيِّ صَلَّى اللَّهُ عَلَيْهِ وَآلِهِ وَسَلَّمَ فِيمَا يَرْوِيهِ عَنْ رَبِّهِ تَبَارَكَ وَتَعَالَى، أَنَّهُ قَالَ:

"يَا عِبَادِي: إنِّي حَرَّمْت الظُّلْمَ عَلَى نَفْسِي، وَجَعَلْته بَيْنَكُمْ مُحَرَّمًا؛ فَلَا تَظَالَمُوا. يَا عِبَادِي! كُلُّكُمْ ضَالٌّ إلَّا مَنْ هَدَيْته، فَاسْتَهْدُونِي أَهْدِكُمْ. يَا عِبَادِي! كُلُّكُمْ جَائِعٌ إلَّا مَنْ أَطْعَمْته، فَاسْتَطْعِمُونِي أُطْعِمْكُمْ. يَا عِبَادِي! كُلُّكُمْ عَارٍ إلَّا مَنْ كَسَوْته، فَاسْتَكْسُونِي أَكْسُكُمْ. يَا عِبَادِي! إنَّكُمْ تُخْطِئُونَ بِاللَّيْلِ وَالنَّهَارِ، وَأَنَا أَغْفِرُ الذُّنُوبَ جَمِيعًا؛ فَاسْتَغْفِرُونِي أَغْفِرْ لَكُمْ. يَا عِبَادِي! إنَّكُمْ لَنْ تَبْلُغُوا ضُرِّي فَتَضُرُّونِي، وَلَنْ تَبْلُغُوا نَفْعِي فَتَنْفَعُونِي. يَا عِبَادِي! لَوْ أَنَّ أَوَّلَكُمْ وَآخِرَكُمْ وَإِنْسَكُمْ وَجِنَّكُمْ كَانُوا عَلَى أَتْقَى قَلْبِ رَجُلٍ وَاحِدٍ مِنْكُمْ، مَا زَادَ ذَلِكَ فِي مُلْكِي شَيْئًا. يَا عِبَادِي! لَوْ أَنَّ أَوَّلَكُمْ وَآخِرَكُمْ وَإِنْسَكُمْ وَجِنَّكُمْ كَانُوا عَلَى أَفْجَرِ قَلْبِ رَجُلٍ وَاحِدٍ مِنْكُمْ، مَا نَقَصَ ذَلِكَ مِنْ مُلْكِي شَيْئًا. يَا عِبَادِي! لَوْ أَنَّ أَوَّلَكُمْ وَآخِرَكُمْ وَإِنْسَكُمْ وَجِنَّكُمْ قَامُوا فِي صَعِيدٍ وَاحِدٍ، فَسَأَلُونِي، فَأَعْطَيْت كُلَّ وَاحِدٍ مَسْأَلَته، مَا نَقَصَ ذَلِكَ مِمَّا عِنْدِي إلَّا كَمَا يَنْقُصُ الْمِخْيَطُ إذَا أُدْخِلَ الْبَحْرَ. يَا عِبَادِي! إنَّمَا هِيَ أَعْمَالُكُمْ أُحْصِيهَا لَكُمْ، ثُمَّ أُوَفِّيكُمْ إيَّاهَا؛ فَمَنْ وَجَدَ خَيْرًا فَلْيَحْمَدْ اللَّهَ، وَمَنْ وَجَدَ غَيْرَ ذَلِكَ فَلَا يَلُومَن إلَّا نَفْسَهُ".

رَوَاهُ مُسْلِمٌ.

On the authority of Abū Dhar Al-Ghiffārī, of the Prophet (pbuh) is that among the sayings he relates from his Lord is that He said,

"O My servants! I have forbidden oppression for Myself, and I have made it forbidden amongst you, so do not oppress one another. O My servants, all of you are astray except those whom I have guided, so seek guidance from Me and I shall guide you. O My servants, all of you are hungry except those whom I have fed, so seek food from Me and I shall feed you. O My servants, all of you are naked except those whom I have clothed, so seek clothing from Me and I shall clothe you. O My servants, you commit sins by day and by night, and I forgive all sins, so seek forgiveness from Me and I shall forgive you. O My servants, you will not attain harming Me so as to harm Me, and you will not attain benefitting Me so as to benefit Me. O My servants, if the first of you and the last of you, and the humans of you and the jinn of you, were all as pious as the most pious heart of any individual amongst you, then this would not increase My Kingdom an iota. O My servants, if the first of you and the last of you, and the humans of you and the jinn of you, were all as wicked as the most wicked heart of any individual amongst you, then this would not decrease My Kingdom an iota. O My servants, if the first of you and the last of you, and the humans of you and the jinn of you, were all to stand together in one place and ask of Me, and I were to give everyone what he requested, then that would not decrease what I Possess, except what is decreased of the ocean when a needle is dipped into it. O My servants, it is but your deeds that I account for you, and then recompense you for. So, he who finds good, let him praise Allah, and he who finds other than that, let him blame no one but himself."

Related by Muslim.

Themes

This *Qudsī*[125] hadith covers a range of profound themes. It holds a

---

[125] For this type of hadith, scholars have two close definitions. The first definition: "Hadith Qudsi refers to the words of God (not included in the Qur'an) transmitted exactly as they are from the mouth of Prophet Muhammad (pbuh), except for the

special place because, through this monologue, God imparts powerful messages, including:

- The recognition of both human and divine realities, highlighting the necessity of connection and dependence on the Creator
- The importance of living in alignment with Divine Guidance

Explanation

From the beginning of this hadith, the Almighty Allah invites and guides humanity to renounce oppression, violence, and injustice. He clarifies that He does not allow oppression upon Himself, so that people understand that when they commit or endure oppression, it is not a result of Allah's anger towards them but rather a consequence of human flaws. Allah states in the Qur'an,

"إِنَّ اللَّهَ لَا يَظْلِمُ النَّاسَ شَيْئًا وَلَٰكِنَّ النَّاسَ أَنفُسَهُمْ يَظْلِمُونَ"

"Indeed, Allah does not wrong people at all, but it is the people who wrong themselves."[126]

This emphasizes that oppression and injustice stem from human imperfections, not from any displeasure of Allah towards humanity.

The Messenger of Allah (pbuh) spoke about injustice, stating, "Injustice will appear as darkness on the Day of Judgment."[127]

Injustice can be categorized into three types:

1. Injustice towards oneself occurs when one mistreats the gifts bestowed by Allah, such as their body and soul. For instance, the use

---

parts where Prophet Muhammad (pbuh) describes God." The second definition: "Hadith Qudsi refers to the words of Muhammad (pbuh), but the meaning comes from Allah (Glorified and Exalted be He) through dreams or divine inspiration." See Ahmad Umar Hashim: *Qawa'id Usul al-Hadith*, Dar al-Kitab al-Arabi, Beirut, 1984, p. 24.

126 Q. (10:44).

127 Shamsuddin al-Kirmani: *Al-Kawakib al-Darari fi Sharh Sahih al-Bukhari*, vol. 11, Hadith 2284, p. 20.

of alcohol or drugs harms the body, constituting self-injustice. The consequences of such sins affect a person both physically and spiritually. Allah and His Messenger (pbuh) have clearly outlined prohibitions to prevent individuals from harming themselves or committing injustice.

2. Injustice towards others encompasses all forms of wrongdoing, violence, and tyranny directed at fellow human beings.

3. Injustice towards the Creator occurs through beliefs in other deities besides Allah or denial of His existence, which constitutes injustice towards Him. However, this injustice does not affect Allah Himself but rather the individual who commits it. The Qur'an states,

"وَلَا تَضُرُّوهُ شَيْئًا وَاللَّهُ عَلَىٰ كُلِّ شَيْءٍ قَدِيرٌ"

"...And you will not harm Him at all, for Allah is All-Powerful over everything."[128]

The following four sentences in continuation of the hadith clearly demonstrate that it is Allah who guides humanity from wrong paths to His straight path, from being unprovided for to being nourished, from being unclothed to being clothed, from sinfulness to being forgiven by His great Mercy. These sentences illustrate the connection of human existence with the Creator, Allah. However, Allah does not distinguish between Himself and humanity to devalue humans, but rather to give them complete value, highlighting that if one believes in the Almighty, worships Him alone, and prays to Him alone, then they will certainly receive His rewards.

In the second sentence, guidance (*al-hidāyah*) is mentioned. According to Mufti Muḥammad Shafī' (d. 1976/1354), there are three different types of guidance:

1. Natural guidance. The sun produces rays of light and warmth. The moon reflects the light of the sun. All these follow a cycle of guidance that Allah has ordained, and this guidance is called "natural guidance." When Prophet Musa (pbuh) was asked by Pharaoh who Allah is,

---

128 Q. (9:39).

"قَالَ رَبُّنَا الَّذِي أَعْطَى كُلَّ شَيْءٍ خَلْقَهُ ثُمَّ هَدَى"

"He said, 'Our Lord is He who gave each thing its form and then guided (it).'"[129]

2. Guidance in faith. The believers who sincerely followed the Messenger of Allah (pbuh) and believed in the words revealed to him have attained guidance in faith.

"الَّذِينَ يَتَّبِعُونَ الرَّسُولَ النَّبِيَّ الْأُمِّيَّ الَّذِي يَجِدُونَهُ مَكْتُوبًا عِندَهُمْ فِي التَّوْرَاةِ وَالْإِنجِيلِ يَأْمُرُهُم بِالْمَعْرُوفِ وَيَنْهَاهُمْ عَنِ الْمُنكَرِ وَيُحِلُّ لَهُمُ الطَّيِّبَاتِ وَيُحَرِّمُ عَلَيْهِمُ الْخَبَائِثَ وَيَضَعُ عَنْهُمْ إِصْرَهُمْ وَالْأَغْلَالَ الَّتِي كَانَتْ عَلَيْهِمْ فَالَّذِينَ آمَنُوا بِهِ وَعَزَّرُوهُ وَنَصَرُوهُ وَاتَّبَعُوا النُّورَ الَّذِي أُنزِلَ مَعَهُ أُولَٰئِكَ هُمُ الْمُفْلِحُونَ"

"Those who follow the Messenger, the unlettered prophet, whom they find mentioned in their scriptures—the Torah and the Gospel—he commands them to do good and forbids them from evil, he allows them lawful things and prohibits for them impure things, and he relieves them of their burdens and the chains that were upon them. So, those who believe in him, honor him, support him, and follow the light which has been sent down with him—they are the successful."[130]

3. Guidance of the heart towards the Divine Reality. This means that the heart of the believer is directed solely towards Allah and to Allah, experiencing with all their being the Unity of Allah (*tawḥīd*) and witnessing the effects of this reality in all of His creations. In the Qur'an, it is said,

"وَالَّذِينَ جَاهَدُوا فِينَا لَنَهْدِيَنَّهُمْ سُبُلَنَا وَإِنَّ اللَّهَ لَمَعَ الْمُحْسِنِينَ"

---

[129] Q. (20:50).

[130] Q. (7:157).

"Those who strive for Us—We will surely guide them to Our ways. And indeed, Allah is with the doers of good."[131,132]

In the aforementioned hadith, Allah emphasizes the importance of repentance for humanity's sins, as He alone forgives them. Allah's love for humanity is evident in their creation, designed to obey Him, love Him, and seek Him in all matters. The Qur'an states,

"وَاللَّهُ يُرِيدُ أَن يَتُوبَ عَلَيْكُمْ وَيُرِيدُ الَّذِينَ يَتَّبِعُونَ الشَّهَوَاتِ أَن تَمِيلُوا مَيْلًا عَظِيمًا ﴿٢٧﴾ يُرِيدُ اللَّهُ أَن يُخَفِّفَ عَنكُمْ وَخُلِقَ الْإِنسَانُ ضَعِيفًا"

"Allah desires to accept your repentance, while those who follow their desires want you to deviate tremendously. Allah intends to lighten your burden, for mankind was created weak."[133]

Furthermore, the hadith emphasizes that humanity cannot benefit Allah directly. Rather, Islamic acts of worship, such as expressing gratitude by saying Praise be to Allah (*alḥamdu lil-lāh*), purify individuals and draw them closer to their Creator. Similarly, affirming "There is no god but Allah" affects the individual's inner self, drawing them nearer to Allah, which leads one closer to all forms of goodness. The Qur'an affirms,

"وَلَقَدْ آتَيْنَا لُقْمَانَ الْحِكْمَةَ أَنِ اشْكُرْ لِلَّهِ وَمَن يَشْكُرْ فَإِنَّمَا يَشْكُرُ لِنَفْسِهِ وَمَن كَفَرَ فَإِنَّ اللَّهَ غَنِيٌّ حَمِيدٌ"

"And We had certainly given Luqman wisdom, (saying), 'Be grateful to Allah.' And whoever is grateful, it is for (the benefit of) himself. And whoever denies (His favor)—then indeed, Allah is Free of need and Praiseworthy."[134]

---

131 Q. (29:69).

132 Muhammad Shafi: Ma'ariful Qur'an; A Comprehensive Commentary on the Holy Quran, Maktaba-e-Darul-Uloom, Karachi, 2020, p. 72-6.

133 Q. (4:27-8).

134 Q. (31:12).

Likewise, those who deny Allah's existence harm only themselves, as affirmed clearly in this verse.

HADITH 25

الحديث الخامس والعشرون

The Virtue of Remembering Allah (*Dhikr*)

عَنْ أَبِي ذَرٍّ أَيْضًا، "أَنَّ نَاسًا مِنْ أَصْحَابِ رَسُولِ اللَّهِ (صَلَّى اللّهُ عَلَيْهِ وَآلِهِ وَسَلَّمَ) قَالُوا لِلنَّبِيِّ (صَلَّى اللّهُ عَلَيْهِ وَآلِهِ وَسَلَّمَ):
"يَا رَسُولَ اللَّهِ ذَهَبَ أَهْلُ الدُّثُورِ بِالْأُجُورِ؛ يُصَلُّونَ كَمَا نُصَلِّي، وَيَصُومُونَ كَمَا نَصُومُ، وَيَتَصَدَّقُونَ بِفُضُولِ أَمْوَالِهِمْ". قَالَ: "أَوَلَيْسَ قَدْ جَعَلَ اللَّهُ لَكُمْ مَا تَصَّدَّقُونَ؟ إنَّ بِكُلِّ تَسْبِيحَةٍ صَدَقَةً، وَكُلِّ تَكْبِيرَةٍ صَدَقَةً، وَكُلِّ تَحْمِيدَةٍ صَدَقَةً، وَكُلِّ تَهْلِيلَةٍ صَدَقَةً، وَأَمْرٌ بِمَعْرُوفٍ صَدَقَةٌ، وَنَهْيٌ عَنْ مُنْكَرٍ صَدَقَةٌ، وَفِي بُضْعِ أَحَدِكُمْ صَدَقَةٌ". قَالُوا: "يَا رَسُولَ اللَّهِ: أَيَأْتِي أَحَدُنَا شَهْوَتَهُ وَيَكُونُ لَهُ فِيهَا أَجْرٌ؟" قَالَ: "أَرَأَيْتُمْ لَوْ وَضَعَهَا فِي حَرَامٍ أَكَانَ عَلَيْهِ وِزْرٌ؟ فَكَذَلِكَ إذَا وَضَعَهَا فِي الْحَلَالِ، كَانَ لَهُ أَجْرٌ".
رَوَاهُ مُسْلِمٌ.

On the authority of Abū Dhar (r.a.):

"Some people from amongst the Companions of the Messenger of Allah (peace be upon him) said to the Prophet (pbuh), 'O Messenger of Allah, the affluent have made off with the rewards; they pray as we pray, they fast as we fast, and they give (much) in charity by virtue of their wealth.' He (pbuh) said, 'Has not Allah made things for you to give in charity? Truly every *tasbīh* (saying *subhān Allāh*) is a charity, and every *takbīr* (saying *Allahu Akbar*) is a charity, and every *tahmīd* (saying *al-*

ḥamdulil-lāh) is a charity, and every *tahlīl* (saying *Lā Ilāha il-lā Allāh*) is a charity. And commanding the good is a charity, and forbidding an evil is a charity, and in the sexual act of each one of you there is a charity.' They said, 'O Messenger of Allah, when one of us fulfills his sexual desire, will he have some reward for that?' He (pbuh) said, 'Do you not see that if he were to act upon it (his desire) in an unlawful manner, then he would be deserving of punishment? Likewise, if he were to act upon it in a lawful manner, then he will be deserving of a reward.'"

Related by Muslim.

Themes

- The commitment of people from all societal layers during the time of Prophet Muhammad (pbuh)
- The significance of engaging in the remembrance of Allah (*dhikr*)
- The directive to perform virtuous deeds and abstain from evil actions
- The profound impact, whether positive or negative, that every action, no matter how ordinary or significant, carries

Explanation

Wealth serves as a test for humanity. When used correctly—thanking the Bestower and distributing it in accordance with Islamic teachings—the believer earns rewards from Allah Almighty. Unfortunately, many among the wealthy are less grateful to God, the Bestower of wealth. Consequently, they fail this test and face His punishment. When Islam is practiced sincerely, especially during the time of Prophet Muhammad (pbuh), people viewed wealth as a divine gift and recognized it as a trial for which they would be held accountable regarding how they earned and distributed it.

One striking aspect of this hadith is how the poor, despite lacking wealth, strive to equal the wealthy in earning rewards from Allah. The Messenger of Allah (pbuh) taught his followers the profound impact of remembering Allah (*dhikr*), likening it to charitable acts.

In another hadith narrated by Abu Hurayrah (r.a.), the Prophet (pbuh) emphasized that the remembrance of Allah holds a status comparable to charity. He advised impoverished immigrants from Mecca that continuous recitation of *Subḥān Allāh*, *al-Ḥamdu li-l-lāh*, and *Allāhu Akbar* would elevate them in goodness.

Beyond the significance of *dhikr*, the Prophet (pbuh) underscored the importance for believers to enjoin good and forbid evil. This fundamental virtue distinguishes Muslims from others. The encouragement of good deeds and the prevention of evil align with the Qur'anic verse where Allah praises Muslims as the best community:

"كُنتُمْ خَيْرَ أُمَّةٍ أُخْرِجَتْ لِلنَّاسِ تَأْمُرُونَ بِالْمَعْرُوفِ وَتَنْهَوْنَ عَنِ الْمُنكَرِ وَتُؤْمِنُونَ بِاللَّهِ"

"You are the best nation produced (as an example) for mankind. You enjoin what is right and forbid what is wrong and believe in Allah."[135]

This approach has not only made Muslim believers beneficial to themselves but also to the societies they inhabit, as they strive to uphold virtues and deter vices.

Finally, in concluding this hadith, the Messenger of Allah (pbuh) mentioned the profound impact of every action, whether perceived as minor or significant. The example given—where even intimate acts with one's spouse may yield rewards—illustrates that seemingly ordinary actions can earn rewards from Allah. This teaching reminds believers that when a legitimate act is performed with good intentions within the bounds of Islam, it carries rewards from Allah, despite appearing trivial. The Prophet (pbuh) enlightens believers about the blessings of deeds, reflecting Allah's mercy, evident through His willingness to bestow rewards for even the simplest acts. As stated in the Qur'an:

---

[135] Q. (3:110).

"يُرِيدُ اللَّهُ أَن يُخَفِّفَ عَنكُمْ وَخُلِقَ الْإِنسَانُ ضَعِيفًا"

"Allah wants to lighten (the burden) for you, and mankind was created weak."[136]

[136] Q. (4:28).

HADITH 26

الحديث السادس والعشرون

Methods of Giving Charity

نْ أَبِي هُرَيْرَةَ رَضِيَ اللهُ عَنْهُ قَالَ: قَالَ رَسُولُ اللَّهِ صلى الله عليه وسلم:
"كُلُّ سُلَامَى مِنْ النَّاسِ عَلَيْهِ صَدَقَةٌ، كُلَّ يَوْمٍ تَطْلُعُ فِيهِ الشَّمْسُ تَعْدِلُ بَيْنَ اثْنَيْنِ
صَدَقَةٌ، وَتُعِينُ الرَّجُلَ فِي دَابَّتِهِ فَتَحْمِلُهُ عَلَيْهَا أَوْ تَرْفَعُ لَهُ عَلَيْهَا مَتَاعَهُ صَدَقَةٌ،
وَالْكَلِمَةُ الطَّيِّبَةُ صَدَقَةٌ، وَبِكُلِّ خُطْوَةٍ تَمْشِيهَا إلَى الصَّلَاةِ صَدَقَةٌ، وَتُمِيطُ الْأَذَى
عَنْ الطَّرِيقِ صَدَقَةٌ".
رَوَاهُ الْبُخَارِيُّ وَمُسْلِمٌ.

Abū Hurayrah (r.a.) reported that the Messenger of Allah (pbuh) said, "Every joint of a person must perform a charity each day that the sun rises: to judge justly between two people is a charity. To help a man with his mount, lifting him onto it or hoisting up his belongings onto it, is a charity. And the good word is a charity. And every step that you take towards prayer is a charity, and removing a harmful object from the road is a charity."

Related by Al-Bukhārī and Muslim.

Theme

- Harnessing the blessings bestowed by Allah to serve His creations and guide them towards His worship

Explanation

Allah Almighty has bestowed numerous blessings upon humanity and desires that through them, humans positively influence others in the service of Him and His creations. Explaining this hadith, Imam Taftāzānī mentions the statement of some great scholars: "All good deeds and the perfection of the path (*tarīq*) are achieved through sincerity with Allah and good behavior towards His creations."[137]

In his book, Jāmic al-ʿUlūm wa al- Ḥikam, the renowned scholar Imam Ibn Rajab al-Ḥanbalī recounts that a man once complained to Jūnus ibn ʿUbayd about his poverty. In response, the scholar posed a series of questions: Could he sell his eyesight, hand, or foot for 100,000 dirhams? Each time, the man replied in the negative. Jūnus ibn ʿUbayd then pointed out the irony that despite possessing considerable wealth, the man continued to complain about his poverty.[138]

This exchange between Jūnus ibn ʿUbayd and the man illustrates that Allah has bestowed upon humans a perfect body, more precious than any wealth, which cannot be traded. Allah does not demand repayment for this gift but expects gratitude and praise from the people. Hence, the Prophet (pbuh) begins the hadith with: "In every joint of the body of man, there is charity (*ṣadaqah*) owed every day that the sun rises."

This hadith also emphasizes that serving Allah's creations should extend beyond specific actions. It includes diverse categories, such as promoting justice among people and removing obstacles from pathways. These acts of charity are expressions of gratitude to Allah, the Bestower of innumerable blessings.

Through this hadith, the Messenger of Allah (pbuh) encourages and instructs his followers to engage in various forms of charity. Such guidance is found in several other hadiths as well. For instance, in a hadith narrated by Abū Dhar (r.a.), the Prophet (pbuh) stated, "When a person wakes up, there is charity due for every joint in his body. Each utterance of Allah's glorification (*tasbih*), praise (*taḥmīd*), declaration of His Oneness (*tahlīl*),

---

137 Sa'd al-Din Masud bin Umar bin Abd Allah: *Sharh al-Taftazani ala al-Arbain al-Nawawiyyah*, p. 168.

138 Zayn al-Din ibn Shihab al-Din: *Jami' al-Ulum wa al-Hikam*, p. 550-1.

and exaltation (*takbīr*) constitutes charity. Commanding good deeds and forbidding evil deeds are also acts of charity. Furthermore, performing two units (*rak'ah*) of the Duḥā[139] prayer suffices for all of these."[140]

The Prophet (pbuh) makes it even easier for those who cannot financially support the needy: to frequently mention Allah (Glorified and Exalted be He). He explains that for them, giving charity is embodied in abstaining from evil deeds.[141]

---

139 Supererogatory prayer in the morning, after the sun rises.

140 Muslim ibn al-Hajjaj: *Sahih Muslim*, vol. 1, p. 325-6.

141 See Shamsuddin al-Kirmani: *Al-Kawakib al-Darari fī Sharh Sahih al-Bukhari*, vol. 7, p. 207-8.

HADITH 27

الحديث السابع والعشرون

The Good and the Bad

عن النَّوَّاسِ بنِ سِمْعانَ رَضِيَ اللهُ عَنْهُ، عَنِ النَّبِيِّ صَلَّى اللهُ عَلَيْهِ وَسَلَّمَ قالَ: "الْبِرُّ حُسْنُ الْخُلُقِ، وَالإِثْمُ مَا حَاكَ فِي نَفْسِكَ وَكَرِهْتَ أَنْ يَطَّلِعَ عليْهِ النَّاسُ".

وعن [وابِصَةَ بنِ مَعْبَدٍ] رَضِيَ اللهُ عَنْهُ قالَ: (أتيتُ رسولَ اللهِ صَلَّى اللهُ عَلَيْهِ وَسَلَّمَ فَقالَ: "جِئْتَ تَسْأَلُ عَنِ الْبِرِّ" قُلْتُ: نَعَمْ. قالَ: "اسْتَفْتِ قَلْبَكَ؛ الْبِرُّ مَا اطْمَأَنَّتْ إِلَيْهِ النَّفْسُ وَاطْمَأَنَّ إِلَيْهِ الْقَلْبُ، وَالإِثْمُ مَا حَاكَ فِي النَّفْسِ وَتَرَدَّدَ فِي الصَّدْرِ وَإِنْ أَفْتَاكَ النَّاسُ وَأَفْتَوْكَ").

حَديثٌ حَسَنٌ رُوِّيناهُ في مُسْنَدَيِ الإمامَيْنِ أحمدَ بنِ حَنْبَلٍ والدَّارِمِيِّ بإسنادٍ حَسَنٍ.

From al-Nawwās bin al-Samʿān (r.a.), from the Prophet (pbuh) that he said,

"Righteousness (*al-birr*) is good morality, and wrongdoing is that which wavers in your soul and which you dislike people finding out about."

And on the authority of Wābiṣah bin Maʿbad (r.a.) that he said: I came to the Messenger of Allah (pbuh) and he said, "You have come to ask about righteousness?" I said, "Yes." He said, "Consult your heart. Righteousness is that about which the soul feels tranquil and the heart feels tranquil, and wrongdoing is that which wavers in the soul and moves to and from in the breast even though people again and again have given you their legal opinion (in its favor)."

A sound hadith transmitted from the compilations of the two imams, Aḥmad b. Ḥanbāl and Al-Dārimī, with a sound chain of authorities.

Theme

- The difference between a good deed and a sin

Explanation

Two hadiths with similar meanings complement each other in their message. In the first hadith, the Messenger of Allah (pbuh) defines the word "*al-birr*" as "good morality." This word along with "*taqwa*" (piety) are closely related, and they enhance each other's meanings.

In Islamic terminology, some words, when used together in a text, take on distinct meanings even though their definitions might overlap. When these words appear in different contexts, they can convey the same concept. For instance, the words "*īmān*" (faith) and "*Islām*" illustrate this. If used together, "*īmān*" refers to belief, while "*Islām*" pertains to the practical pillars of the faith. However, when these words are used separately, they both generally signify belief. Similarly, "*al-birr*" and "*taqwa,*" when used in the same context, denote purity from sins and fear of Allah, respectively. In different texts, they collectively signify piety.

In the Noble Qur'an, *al-birr* appears in various verses. One such verse details *al-birr*, teaching believers the true practice of goodness and righteous behavior. Allah the Exalted commands,

"لَّيْسَ الْبِرَّ أَن تُوَلُّوا وُجُوهَكُمْ قِبَلَ الْمَشْرِقِ وَالْمَغْرِبِ وَلَكِنَّ الْبِرَّ مَنْ آمَنَ بِاللَّهِ وَالْيَوْمِ الْآخِرِ وَالْمَلَائِكَةِ وَالْكِتَابِ وَالنَّبِيِّينَ وَآتَى الْمَالَ عَلَى حُبِّهِ ذَوِي الْقُرْبَى وَالْيَتَامَى وَالْمَسَاكِينَ وَابْنَ السَّبِيلِ وَالسَّائِلِينَ وَفِي الرِّقَابِ وَأَقَامَ الصَّلَاةَ وَآتَى الزَّكَاةَ وَالْمُوفُونَ بِعَهْدِهِمْ إِذَا عَاهَدُوا وَالصَّابِرِينَ فِي الْبَأْسَاءِ وَالضَّرَّاءِ وَحِينَ الْبَأْسِ أُولَئِكَ الَّذِينَ صَدَقُوا وَأُولَئِكَ هُمُ الْمُتَّقُونَ"

"Righteousness is not that you turn your faces toward the east or the west, but (true) righteousness is (in) one who believes in Allah, the Last

Day, the Angels, the Book, and the Prophets and gives his wealth, in spite of love for it, to relatives, orphans, the needy, the traveler, those who ask (for help), and for freeing slaves; (and who) establishes prayer and gives zakah; (those who) fulfill their promise when they promise; and (those who) are patient in poverty and hardship and during battle. Those are the ones who have been true, and it is those who are the righteous."[142]

Commenting on *al-birr*, the renowned hadith scholar, Imam Muḥammad bin ʿĪsā al-Tirmidhī, explains, "In this hadith, *al-birr* encompasses the maintenance of family ties, acts of benevolence, and obedience. All these qualities are included within the broader concept of good conduct (*ḥusn al-khuluq*)."[143]

The second hadith shares a similar purpose with the first but differs in content. In it, the Messenger of Allah (pbuh) advises the questioner to consult their heart when determining what constitutes a sin or something disliked, because the heart, which is central to human nature, reflects and confirms Divine Revelation, the Qur'an. In this context, it refers to a heart attuned to the Creator. For instance, if Allah forbids backbiting, a person's heart will not feel at ease and will experience anxiety when committing this sin. The same principle applies to other sins.

The hadith further emphasizes that even if people, including those issuing hastened non-binding Islamic legal opinions (*fatwa*), express their views in favor of an action that is actually sinful, a believer should refrain from that action if they feel discomfort in their heart.

---

[142] Q. (2:177).

[143] See Sa'd al-Din Masud bin Umar bin Abdallah: *Sharh al-Taftazani ala al-Arbain al-Nawawiyyah*, p. 169.

HADITH 28

الحديث الثامن والعشرون

Following the Prophetic Tradition (Sunnah) and the Rightly Guided Caliphs

عَنْ أَبي نَجِيحِ العِرْباضِ بنِ سَارِيةَ رَضِي اللهُ عَنْهُ قالَ: (وَعَظَنا رَسُولُ اللهِ صَلَّى اللهُ عَلَيْهِ وَسَلَّمَ مَوْعِظَةً وَجِلَتْ مِنْها القُلوبُ، وَذَرَفَتْ مِنْها العُيُونُ، فَقُلْنا: يا رسولَ اللهِ، كَأَنَّها مَوْعِظَةُ مُودِّعٍ فَأَوْصِنا. قالَ: "أُوصِيكُمْ بِتَقْوى اللهِ عَزَّ وَجَلَّ، وَالسَّمْعِ وَالطَّاعَةِ، وَإِنْ تَأَمَّرَ عَلَيْكُمْ عَبْدٌ حَبَشِيٌّ، فَإِنَّهُ مَنْ يَعِشْ مِنْكُمْ فَسَيَرَى اخْتِلافًا كَثِيرًا، فَعَلَيْكُمْ بِسُنَّتِي وَسُنَّةِ الْخُلَفَاءِ الرَّاشِدِينَ الْمَهْدِيِّينَ، تَمَسَّكُوا بِها، وَعَضُّوا عَلَيْها بِالنَّواجِذِ، وَإِيَّاكُمْ وَمُحْدَثاتِ الأُمُورِ؛ فَإِنَّ كُلَّ مُحْدَثَةٍ بِدْعَةٌ، وَكُلَّ بِدْعَةٍ ضَلالَةٌ".

رواهُ أبو داوُدَ والتِّرمِذِيُّ، وقالَ: حديثٌ حَسَنٌ صحيحٌ.

It was narrated on the authority of Abū Najīḥ al-ʿIrbāḍ bin Sāriyah (r.a.) who said,

The Messenger of Allah (pbuh) delivered an admonition that made our hearts fearful and our eyes tearful. We said, "O Messenger of Allah, it is as if this were a farewell sermon, so advise us." He said, "I enjoin you to have Taqwa of Allah and that you listen and obey, even if a slave is made a ruler over you. He among you who lives long enough will see many differences. So for you is to observe my Sunnah and the Sunnah of the rightly-principled and rightly-guided successors, holding on to them with your molar teeth. Beware of newly-introduced matters, for every innovation (*bid ʿah*) is an error."

Related by Abū Dāwūd and Al-Tirmidhī, who say it is a reliable-authentic hadith (*ḥasan-sahīḥ*).

Themes

- Unwavering devotion
- Loyalty to leaders
- Commitment to prophetic tradition and the rightly guided Caliphs
- Rejection of religious innovations (*bid ʿah*)

Explanation

Abū Najīḥ al-ʿIrbāḍ bin Sāriyah (r.a.), the narrator of this hadith, was one of the "People of the Bench" (*ahl al-suffa*)[144], known for their profound love for the Messenger of Allah (pbuh). This deep affection is vividly captured by the narrator's words: "Hearts were illuminated and eyes wept." As Imam Ibn Rajab al-Ḥanbalī explains, the feelings and qualities of such people are described in this Qur'anic verse[145]:

"إِنَّمَا الْمُؤْمِنُونَ الَّذِينَ إِذَا ذُكِرَ اللَّهُ وَجِلَتْ قُلُوبُهُمْ وَإِذَا تُلِيَتْ عَلَيْهِمْ آيَاتُهُ زَادَتْهُمْ إِيمَانًا وَعَلَىٰ رَبِّهِمْ يَتَوَكَّلُونَ"

[144] Suffa was a place in the rear part of the Prophet's (pbuh) Mosque, covered by a roof. There, the poor believers and those without homes stayed. These believers were known for their intense love for the Messenger of Allah (pbuh), their devotion, and their continuous remembrance of Allah day and night. Some of them transmitted numerous hadiths of the Prophet (pbuh), such as Abu Hurayrah (r.a.). In fact, this companion holds the first place in transmitting hadiths, even before the Prophet's wife Aisha (may Allah be pleased with her). Some of the other names included: Abu Dhar al-Ghifari, Abdullah ibn Mas'ud, Salman al-Farisi, Ka'b ibn Malik, Abu Sa'id al-Khudri, Bilal ibn Rabah, Suhayb al-Rumi, and others.

[145] Zayn al-Din bin Shihab al-Din: *Jamia' al-Ulum wa al-Hikam*, p. 584.

"True believers are those whose hearts tremble when Allah is mentioned, and when His revelations are recited to them, it strengthens their faith, and they rely upon their Lord."[146]

The Messenger of Allah (pbuh) then advises his followers to be devoted to Islam, as devotion or righteousness (*taqwā*) is the foundation of worship.[147]

He also instructs believers to be obedient and to submit to their leader, even if he is a servant. By using an unconventional example, the Messenger of Allah (pbuh) emphasizes that people should not judge their leaders based on social status, but rather on their service to the people. Obedience to and compliance with rulers prevent division among the people and ensure peace. This does not refer to rulers who openly sin and disregard the teachings of the Qur'an, but to those who lead according to Islamic principles. The Messenger of Allah (pbuh) said, "O people! Fear Allah! If a mutilated Ethiopian slave is appointed as your leader and he rules you with the Book of Allah, then listen to him and obey him."[148]

The hadith also mentions that those who live long from the generation of the Prophet Muhammad (pbuh) will witness many contradictions. Indeed, this came true. Due to the conflicts and hostilities of certain groups against the leaders of the believers, three of them (caliphs) were martyred in different years, and unjustly killed in cold blood. They were ʿUmar, ʿUthmān, and ʿAlī (may Allah be pleased with them). This accurate prediction by the Prophet (pbuh) is considered a prophetic miracle, as no one could have known such events would occur.

Additionally, in this hadith, the Prophet (pbuh) emphasizes the importance of adhering to his tradition (*sunnah*) and that of his caliphs. A believer cannot be rightly guided without following the prophetic tradition and teachings. The Prophet's (pbuh) example is essential for implementing Qur'anic teachings. Allah sent Prophet Muhammad (pbuh)

---

[146] Q. (8:2).

[147] See the explanation of Hadith 18 in this book, which contains detailed information regarding righteousness, *taqwa*.

[148] Abu Isa al-Tirmidhi, *Al-Jami' al-Sahih*, published by Mustafa al-Babi al-Halabi wa Awladuh, Cairo, 1962, vol. 1, pg 209.

to demonstrate how to put divine teachings into practice. In the Qur'an, Allah clearly highlights the significance of the Prophet's (pbuh) life for believers:

"لَّقَدْ كَانَ لَكُمْ فِي رَسُولِ اللَّهِ أُسْوَةٌ حَسَنَةٌ لِّمَن كَانَ يَرْجُو اللَّهَ وَالْيَوْمَ الْآخِرَ وَذَكَرَ اللَّهَ كَثِيرًا"

"Certainly, you have in the Messenger of Allah an excellent example for anyone who hopes in Allah and the Last Day and remembers Allah often."[149]

Following the tradition of the caliphs is also crucial because they faithfully followed the Prophet's (pbuh) path, making judgments and guiding others based on divine teachings. Hence, the Messenger of Allah (pbuh) referred to them as rightly guided (*al-rashidūn*) and those on the right path (*al-mahdiyyīn*).

In conclusion, the Prophet (pbuh) advises believers to avoid innovations in religion (*bid ʿah*). The term *bid ʿah* is often misunderstood because scholars have provided various definitions and interpretations. Islamic jurisprudence scholars, like Imam al-Nawawī and others, generally categorize *bid ʿah* into two types: good innovation (*bid ʿah ḥasanah*) and bad innovation (*bid ʿah qabīḥah*). Good innovations include fields such as the Principles of Hadith (*uṣūl al-hadīth*), Islamic Legal Principles (*uṣūl al-fiqh*), and Principles of Qur'anic Interpretation (*uṣūl al-tafsīr*).[150] Bad innovations, on the other hand, are those that do not conform to Qur'anic teachings and the prophetic tradition.

Taqī ad-Dīn Aḥmad ibn Taymiyyah (d. 728/1328), in his book Iqtiḍā Ṣirat al-Mustaqīm, defines *bidʿah* specifically as a bad innovation. He notes that if an innovation is grounded in the Qur'an and the prophetic tradition, it is considered a linguistic innovation (*bidʿah lughawiyyah*) rather than an actionable one, as it is rooted in faith and does not lead believers astray. Examples of bidʿah lughawiyyah he cites include

---

[149] Q. (33:21).

[150] Muhyiddin al-Nawawi: *Tahdhib al-Asma wa al-Lughat*, Dar al-Kutub al-Ilmiyyah, Beirut, (no publishing year available) vol. 3, p. 22.

compiling the Qur'an into a single book after the Prophet's (pbuh) death and the congregational Tarāwīḥ prayer established by the second caliph, cUmar ibn al-Khaṭṭāb (r.a.).[151]

Ibn Taymiyyah's theoretical perspective on innovation in Islam may differ, but in practice, it aligns with the understanding of other traditional and classical Muslim scholars. However, this nuanced view has often been misinterpreted by literalist Muslims, leading them to label many Muslims as people of *bid 'ah*, even when they are within the frame of the Qur'an and the prophetic tradition.

[151] Taqi al-Din Ahmad ibn Taymiyyah: *Iqtida Sirat al-Mustaqim*, Maktabah al-Rushd, Riyadh, (2006) vol. 1, p. 44-5.

HADITH 29

الحديث التاسع والعشرون

Paths to Paradise

عَنْ مُعَاذِ بْنِ جَبَلٍ رَضِيَ اللهُ عَنْهُ قَالَ: قُلْت يَا رَسُولَ اللَّهِ! أَخْبِرْنِي بِعَمَلٍ يُدْخِلُنِي الْجَنَّةَ وَيُبَاعِدْنِي مِنْ النَّارِ، قَالَ:
لَقَدْ سَأَلْت عَنْ عَظِيمٍ، وَإِنَّهُ لَيَسِيرٌ عَلَى مَنْ يَسَّرَهُ اللَّهُ عَلَيْهِ: تَعْبُدُ اللَّهَ لَا تُشْرِكْ بِهِ شَيْئًا، وَتُقِيمُ الصَّلَاةَ، وَتُؤْتِي الزَّكَاةَ، وَتَصُومُ رَمَضَانَ، وَتَحُجُّ الْبَيْتَ، ثُمَّ قَالَ: أَلَا أَدُلُّك عَلَى أَبْوَابِ الْخَيْرِ؟ الصَّوْمُ جُنَّةٌ، وَالصَّدَقَةُ تُطْفِئُ الْخَطِيئَةَ كَمَا يُطْفِئُ الْمَاءُ النَّارَ، وَصَلَاةُ الرَّجُلِ فِي جَوْفِ اللَّيْلِ، ثُمَّ تَلَا: "تتجَافَى جُنُوبُهُمْ عَنِ الْمَضَاجِعِ" حَتَّى بَلَغَ "يَعْمَلُونَ"، سورة السجدة / الأيتان: ١٦ و ١٧] ثُمَّ قَالَ: أَلَا أُخْبِرُك بِرَأْسِ الْأَمْرِ وَعَمُودِهِ وَذُرْوَةِ سَنَامِهِ؟ قُلْت: بَلَى يَا رَسُولَ اللَّهِ. قَالَ: رَأْسُ الْأَمْرِ الْإِسْلَامُ، وَعَمُودُهُ الصَّلَاةُ، وَذُرْوَةُ سَنَامِهِ الْجِهَادُ، ثُمَّ قَالَ: أَلَا أُخْبِرُك بِمَلَاكِ ذَلِكَ كُلِّهِ؟ فقُلْت: بَلَى يَا رَسُولَ اللَّهِ! فَأَخَذَ بِلِسَانِهِ وَقَالَ: كُفَّ عَلَيْك هَذَا. قُلْت: يَا نَبِيَّ اللَّهِ وَإِنَّا لَمُؤَاخَذُونَ بِمَا نَتَكَلَّمُ بِهِ؟ فَقَالَ: ثَكِلَتْك أُمُّك وَهَلْ يَكُبُّ النَّاسَ عَلَى وُجُوهِهِمْ -أَوْ قَالَ عَلَى مَنَاخِرِهِمْ- إلَّاحَصَائِدُ أَلْسِنَتِهِمْ؟

رَوَاهُ التِّرْمِذِيُّ وَقَالَ: حَدِيثٌ حَسَنٌ صَحِيحٌ.

On the authority of Muʿādh bin Jabal (r.a.), who said:

I said, "O Messenger of Allah, tell me of an act which will take me into Paradise and will keep me away from the Hellfire." He (pbuh) said, "You have asked me about a great matter, yet it is easy for him for whom Allah makes it easy. Worship Allah without associating any partners with Him; establish the prayer (*ṣalāh*); pay the almsgiving (*zakāh*); fast in Ramadan; and make the pilgrimage (*ḥajj*) to the House."

Then he (pbuh) said, "Shall I not guide you towards the means of goodness? Fasting is a shield, charity wipes away sin as water extinguishes fire, and the praying of a man in the depths of the night." Then he (peace be upon him) recited: "'(Those) who forsake their beds, to invoke their Lord in fear and hope, and they spend (charity in Allah's cause) out of what We have bestowed on them. No person knows what is kept hidden for them of joy as a reward for what they used to do.'" (Surah al-Sajdah: 16-17).

Then he (pbuh) said, "Shall I not inform you of the head of the matter, its pillar and its peak?" I said, "Yes, O Messenger of Allah." He (peace be upon him) said, "The head of the matter is Islam, its pillar is the prayer and its peak is *jihād*." Then he (pbuh) said, "Shall I not tell you of the foundation of all of that?" I said, "Yes, O Messenger of Allah." So he took hold of his tongue and said, "Restrain this." I said, "O Prophet of Allah, will we be taken to account for what we say with it?" He (peace be upon him) said, "May your mother be bereaved of you, O Muʿādh! Is there anything that throws people into the Hellfire upon their faces, or on their noses, except the harvests of their tongues?"

Related by al-Tirmidhī who mentioned that the hadith is sound/ authentic.

Themes

- Various pathways leading to attaining Paradise
- The human tongue, a primary factor determining one's journey either towards Paradise or towards Hellfire

Explanation

This hadith, akin to those of the Sixteenth and Twenty-Eighth, underscores the deep devotion of the Companions in seeking guidance from the Messenger of Allah (pbuh). It also highlights their dedication to acquiring knowledge and performing deeds that pave the way to Paradise.

The initial counsel given by the Prophet (pbuh) to his companion Muʿādh bin Jabal (r.a.) holds profound significance, addressing the crucial matter of distancing oneself from Hellfire and drawing nearer to Paradise. The Prophet (pbuh) advises steadfast adherence to the pillars of Islam—such as prayer, fasting, charity, and pilgrimage—as these are the means through which Paradise is attained. Despite being well-versed in these fundamentals, some Muslims occasionally shift their focus to secondary matters, losing sight of their commitment to these foundational aspects.

Additionally, the Prophet (pbuh) emphasizes that fasting serves as a protective shield. Observing fasting during Ramadan entails more than abstaining from food and drink; it requires distancing oneself from vices like lying, backbiting, foul language, and idle pursuits. Fasting aids in refraining from sinful acts and fosters a closer connection with the Creator through devotion. Hence, the Prophet describes fasting as a shield against evil deeds.

The virtues of charity and night prayer are also extolled. These acts not only draw believers closer to Allah by subduing the ego, a common barrier in the Creator-creation relationship, but they also exemplify sincerity. Charity and night prayer, often performed in private without seeking public recognition, are sincere acts that steer clear of hypocrisy or worldly gain. Such deeds, performed sincerely for Allah's sake, yield immense rewards and facilitate forgiveness of sins. Allah mentions in the Qur'an,

"وَأَقِمِ الصَّلَاةَ طَرَفَيِ النَّهَارِ وَزُلَفًا مِّنَ اللَّيْلِ إِنَّ الْحَسَنَاتِ يُذْهِبْنَ السَّيِّئَاتِ ذَٰلِكَ ذِكْرَىٰ لِلذَّاكِرِينَ"

"And establish prayer at the two ends of the day and at the approach of the night. Indeed, good deeds do away with misdeeds. That is a reminder for those who remember."[152]

Moreover, the Prophet (pbuh) informs Muʿādh bin Jabal (r.a.) that

[152] Q. (11:114).

the foundation of everything is Islam, emphasizing the testimony of faith (*shahādah*) that there is no deity except Allah and that Muhammad (pbuh) is His Messenger. He reiterates that prayer is the pillar of everything, stressing its importance as he did in another hadith: "The first thing for which a person will be brought to account on the Day of Judgment is prayer."[153]

The Messenger of Allah (pbuh) explains that striving in the path of God (*jihād*) is the pinnacle, or the highest form, of all actions. Just as the roof of a building is its highest part, protecting its inhabitants from the elements, striving in the path of God shields a person from various worldly harms and from their own ego. Often, the word *jihād*, which appears in this hadith and many verses of the Holy Qur'an, is mistakenly interpreted by many as merely physical warfare. This narrow view diminishes the true essence of the term. While fighting an enemy can be a form of *jihād*, the word's meaning extends far beyond that.

Imam Taftazānī, in his commentary on this hadith, explains that *jihād* includes the struggle against external enemies to keep the religion of God pure. More importantly, it also encompasses the internal struggle against one's own ego. According to Imam Taftazānī, this internal struggle is more challenging than the physical one. Hence, the Messenger of Allah (pbuh), upon returning from a battle, stated, "You have come from the lesser *jihād* to the greater *jihād*." When asked what the greater *jihād* was, he replied, "The servant of God's struggle against his own desires."[154]

Imam Taftazānī also highlights another form of *jihād*: the effort of purifying one's heart. This involves severing attachments to anything other than Allah, filling the heart with devotion to God and distancing it from worldly distractions. The *jihād* of the soul involves merging a person's existence with the Existence of the Sole Sovereign, Allah. Through this explanation, Imam Taftazānī illustrates the multifaceted nature of *jihād*, showing that it cannot be confined to fighting with swords or weapons. The term "holy war," often associated with *jihād*, was historically used by

---

153 Tirmidhi: *Al-Jami' al-Sahih*, vol. 2, hadith 413.

154 Abi Bakr Ahmad ibn Husayn al-Bayhaqi: *Kitab al-Zuhd al-Kabir*, 1st ed. Dar al-Jinan, Beirut, 1987, p. 165.

the Crusaders in their battles against Muslims and people of other faiths, further distorting its true meaning.[155]

In the book *Fatḥ al-Rabbānī wa al-Fayḍ al-Raḥmānī*, the renowned Shaikh Abd al-Qādir al-Jaylānī (d. 561/1166) discusses the human ego, stating, "A person's ego (*nafs*) is the inner king, and the army of this king consists of animalistic vices, bad nature, whims, and greed. Consequently, it remains blind, unable to perceive destruction or distinguish between good and evil. This state persists until Allah, with His grace and wisdom, illuminates the ego, enabling the person to clearly see enemies and friends. Only then can the reconstruction of the inner self begin, which was previously filled with the envy of the pig, the savagery of the dog, and the anger of the tiger."[156]

At the end of this hadith, Prophet Muhammad (pbuh) stresses that maintaining faith and Islamic practice is achieved by controlling one's speech. This is a powerful message. The tongue has the power to undermine the honor and respect of others, and it is vital to realize that God has connected faith with how we make others feel, as words can provoke intense emotions. Offensive or false words can easily degrade another person, causing significant harm, oppression, humiliation, and most importantly, God's displeasure. What value does proper worship have if the worshiper simultaneously insults others? Prophet Muhammad (pbuh) said, "If a person does not abandon bad speech (including lies, bad words, gossip, etc.) and bad behavior during fasting, then Allah has no need for his abstention from food and drink."[157]

Muʿādh (r.a.) was astonished by the importance the Messenger of Allah (pbuh) placed on the words people express. The Prophet (pbuh) explained that those who do not control their speech and speak recklessly will face severe punishment in Hell. If we reflect deeply, we will realize that the sin of speaking is easily committed because it requires little effort. Therefore,

---

[155] See Taftazani: *Sharh al-Taftazani ala al-Arbain al-Nawawiyyah*, p. 186.

[156] Abd al-Qadir al-Jaylani: *Al-Fat-h al-Rabbani wa al-Fayd al-Rahmani,* Dar el-Elbab, Bejrut, (no publishing year available).

[157] Al-Bukhārī: *Sahih al-Bukhari*, vol. 9, p. 86-7.

this sin can quickly surpass all others. For this reason, it is mentioned by our Muslim predecessors,

"مَنْ عَرَفَ اَللَّهَ كَلَّ لِسَانُهُ"

"Whoever knows Allah, their tongue becomes restrained."[158]

---

[158] Abu Bakr Al-Jurjani, *The Wisdom of the Sufis: Collection of Mystical Sayings*, trans. A. Ezzati (Oxford: OneWorld Publications, 1996), p. 38.

HADITH 30

الحديث الثلاثون

Observing Islamic Regulations

عَنْ أَبِي ثَعْلَبَةَ الْخُشَنِيِّ جُرْثُومِ بن نَاشِبٍ عَنْ رَسُولِ اللَّهِ صَلَّى اللهُ عَلَيْهِ وَسَلَّمَ قَال: "إِنَّ اللَّهَ تَعَالَى فَرَضَ فَرَائِضَ فَلَا تُضَيِّعُوهَا، وَحَدَّ حُدُودًا فَلَا تَعْتَدُوهَا، وَحَرَّمَ أَشْيَاءَ فَلَا تَنْتَهِكُوهَا، وَسَكَتَ عَنْ أَشْيَاءَ رَحْمَةً لَكُمْ غَيْرَ نِسْيَانٍ فَلَا تَبْحَثُوا عَنْهَا".
حَدِيثٌ حَسَنٌ، رَوَاهُ الدَّارَقُطْنِيّ وَغَيْرُهُ.

On the authority of Abū Thaʿlabah al-Khushʿanī Jurthūm bin Nāshib (r.a.) that the Messenger of Allah (pbuh) said,

"Verily Allah the Almighty has laid down religious obligations (*farā'id*), so do not neglect them. He has set boundaries, so do not overstep them. He has prohibited some things, so do not violate them; about some things He was silent, out of compassion for you, not forgetfulness, so seek not after them."

A reliable hadith, related by Dār al-Qutnī and others.

Themes

- Fulfilling obligations
- Staying within the boundaries set by Allah
- Avoiding unnecessary intricacies

Explanation

This hadith is fundamentally about understanding Islam through adherence to what is permitted and avoidance of what is prohibited. It guides believers on how to attain success with the Creator of the universe.

Neglecting any obligatory act without a valid reason is a sin, and one will be held accountable for it on the Day of Judgment. Some obligatory acts include:

1. Performing the five daily prayers (*salāh*).
2. Fasting during the month of Ramadan.
3. Giving *zakāt* (almsgiving). If a person has reached the minimum threshold of wealth (*niṣāb*) and does not pay *zakāt*, this neglect is considered a sin.

Performing Ḥajj (pilgrimage). Similarly, if a Muslim has the financial and physical ability to perform Ḥajj during their lifetime but neglects it, this neglect is considered a sin.

The Messenger of Allah (pbuh) further states, "Allah has set boundaries, so do not transgress them..." This means that certain actions have been made forbidden (*ḥarām*) for humans, such as worshiping anyone other than Allah, consuming alcohol, eating pork, gambling, engaging in premarital sexual relations, consuming blood, stealing, backbiting, lying, etc. Committing these acts is prohibited and recorded as sins. However, Allah is Merciful, and if He wills, He forgives those who worship none but Him and sincerely seek His forgiveness, resolving not to repeat the sin.

At the end of the hadith, the Messenger of Allah (pbuh) advises believers not to delve into unnecessary details by prohibiting actions that Allah and His Messenger (pbuh) have not specified, or by permitting that which is prohibited. Overemphasizing non-essential matters can lead to neglecting the primary ones, causing an imbalance. Ibn Rajab mentions another similar hadith, explaining that those who concern themselves with irrelevant matters are lost, as are those who focus only on the superficial aspects of words.[159] In another hadith reported by ʿUmar ibn al-Khṭṭāb, the Messenger of Allah (pbuh) said,

---

[159] Zayn al-Din bin Shihab al-Din: *Jami' al-Ulum wa al-Hikam*, p. 636.

"إِيَّاكُمْ وَالتَّعَمُّقَ فِي الدِّينِ؛ فَإِنَّ اللَّهَ عَزَّ وَجَلَّ قَدْ جَعَلَهُ سَهْلًا، فَخُذُوا مِنْهُ مَا تُطِيقُونَ، فَإِنَّ اللَّهَ عَزَّ وَجَلَّ يُحِبُّ مَا دَامَ مِنْ عَمَلٍ صَالِحٍ وَإِنْ كَانَ يَسِيرًا"

"Beware of going to extremes in religion, for Allah has made it easy. Take from the religion what you can handle, for indeed Allah loves consistent good deeds, even if they are small."[160]

---

160 Abu al-Qasim ibn Bishran al-Baghdadi, *Amali ibn Bishran*, Dar al-Vatan, Riyadh, 1997, p. 49.

HADITH 31

الحديث الحادي والثلاثون

The Reality of Asceticism (*Zuhd*)

عَنْ أَبِي الْعَبَّاسِ سَهْلِ بْنِ سَعْدٍ السَّاعِدِيِّ رَضِيَ اللهُ عَنْهُ قَالَ: جَاءَ رَجُلٌ إِلَى النَّبِيِّ صَلَّى اللهُ عَلَيْهِ وَسَلَّمَ فَقَالَ: "يَا رَسُولَ اللهِ! دُلَّنِي عَلَى عَمَلٍ إِذَا عَمِلْتُهُ أَحَبَّنِي اللهُ وَأَحَبَّنِي النَّاسُ"؛ فَقَالَ: "ازْهَدْ فِي الدُّنْيَا يُحِبَّك اللهُ، وَازْهَدْ فِيمَا عِنْدَ النَّاسِ يُحِبَّك النَّاسُ".

حديث حسن، رَوَاهُ ابْنُ مَاجَهْ، وَغَيْرُهُ بِأَسَانِيدَ حَسَنَةٍ.

On the authority of Abī ʿAbbās Sahl bin Saʿad al-Sāʿidī (r.a.) who said: A man came to the Prophet (pbuh) and said: "O Messenger of Allah, direct me to an act which, if I do it, (will cause) Allah to love me and the people to love me." So he (peace be upon him) said, "Renounce the world and Allah will love you, and renounce what people possess and the people will love you."

A reliable hadith, related by Ibn Mājah and others through their reliable chains of narrations.

Theme

- Incorporating asceticism (*zuhd*) in relations with people

Explanation

In this hadith, the Messenger of Allah (pbuh) emphasizes the importance of asceticism (*zuhd*), a virtue bestowed by the Almighty upon believers who strive to detach themselves from unnecessary worldly pleasures and seek to purify their hearts of everything except Allah, constantly feeling His presence. This virtue is often internal and not easily observed by others, as it exists between a person and their Creator. Ibn Rajab mentions that Abū Sulaymān remarked, "You cannot witness someone's *zuhd*, as *zuhd* resides in the heart."[161]

Scholars have defined zuhd in various ways. The Islamic mystic and scholar Abū Bakr al-Kalābādhī (d. 380/990) writes in his book *Al-Ta'arruf li-Madhhab Ahl al-Tasawwuf*: "When Alī (r.a.) was asked about *zuhd*, he replied, '*Zuhd* means not worrying about who benefits from this world, whether they are a believer or a non-believer.'"[162] This means that one should not envy others who pursue worldly possessions but should remain distant from such pursuits, engaging with the world only as necessary and ensuring that worldly matters do not come between them and the Creator. This explanation relates to the first part of the hadith, where the Messenger of Allah (pbuh) indicates that to gain Allah's love, one must distance oneself from worldly greed.

Also, in his book Al-Risālah, Imam al-Qushayrī cites the eminent scholar among the early generation of Muslims, Al-Fuḍayl ibn 'Iyāḍ (d. 187/803), who said, "Allah has placed all evil in a house and made its key the love of this world. He has also placed all good in a house and made its key asceticism (*zuhd*)."[163]

It is also mentioned that Abū Ḥāzim al-Zāhid (d. 139/757) was asked, "What wealth do you possess?" He responded, "I have two types of wealth that protect me from poverty: faith in Allah and losing hope in what people possess." When asked if he feared poverty, he replied, "How can I fear when my Lord owns everything in the heavens, the earth, all

---

[161] Zayn al-Din bin Shihab al-Din: *Jami' al-Ulum wa al-Hikam*, p.644.

[162] Abu Bakr al-Kalabadhi: *Al-Ta'arruf li madhhab ahl al-Tasawwuf*, Dar al-Kutub al-'Ilmiyyah, Beirut, 1993, p. 109.

[163] Abu al-Qasim al-Qushayri: *Al-Risalah al-Qushayriyyah*, p. 223.

between them, and beneath the earth?"[164]

According to Ibn Rajab, zuhd is divided into three categories:

1. Believing that what is in Allah's hands is more secure than what is in one's own.

2. Preferring the rewards (from patience) for any worldly loss, such as wealth or children, over possessing the entire world.

3. Maintaining balance in the face of praise or humiliation, ensuring stability whether praised or criticized, as people often struggle with accepting criticism.[165]

In the second part of the hadith, the Prophet Muhammad (pbuh) mentions that gaining the love of people is also achieved by not coveting what others possess. Greed for wealth and materialism drives individuals to acquire it dishonestly and through lies, leading to competition over material goods. This can cause them to borrow money they cannot repay, resulting in a loss of respect and authority and alienating people from them. Therefore, the Messenger of Allah (pbuh) advised believers to stay away from materialistic greed and coveting others' possessions. People appreciate and love those who resist greed and do not compete for worldly possessions, as they recognize that greed is a human weakness and those who overcome it demonstrate self-restraint over their desires.

---

[164] Zayn al-Din ibn Shihab al-Din: *Jami' al-'Ulum wa al-Hikam*, p. 644.

[165] Ibid.

HADITH 32

الحديث الثاني والثلاثون

Prohibition of Harm

عَنْ أَبِي سَعِيدٍ سَعْدِ بْنِ مَالِكِ بْنِ سِنَانٍ الْخُدْرِيِّ رَضِيَ اللهُ عَنْهُ أَنَّ رَسُولَ اللَّهِ صَلَّى اللهُ عَلَيْهِ وَسَلَّمَ قَالَ: "لَا ضَرَرَ وَلَا ضِرَارَ".

حَدِيثٌ حَسَنٌ، رَوَاهُ ابْنُ مَاجَهْ، وَالدَّارَقُطْنِيّ، وَغَيْرُهُمَا مُسْنَدًا. وَرَوَاهُ مَالِكٌ فِي "الْمُوَطَّإِ" عَنْ عَمْرِو بْنِ يَحْيَى عَنْ أَبِيهِ عَنْ النَّبِيِّ مُرْسَلًا، فَأَسْقَطَ أَبَا سَعِيدٍ، وَلَهُ طُرُقٌ يُقَوِّي بَعْضُهَا بَعْضًا.

It was related on the authority of Abū Sacīd Sa ͑d bin Mālik bin Sinān al-Khuḍrī (r.a.) that the Messenger of Allah (pbuh) said,

"There should be neither harming nor reciprocating harm."

A reliable hadith which Ibn Mājah, Al-Dar Qutnī and others related with a line of transmission (*isnād*). Also, Mālik related in his Muwaṭṭa' with a broken chain, from ͑Amr bin Yaḥyā, from his father, from the Prophet (pbuh) but dropping (the name of) Abū Sacīd. This hadith has lines of transmission which strengthen one another.

Theme

- Prevention of harm

Explanation

This hadith, although concise, holds profound significance. Scholars have offered various interpretations of its meaning. Some interpret the word "harm" (*ḍarar*) as an act committed for personal gain at the expense of others, while the word "to harm" (*ḍirār*) refers to an act that brings no benefit but only causes harm to others.[166]

For instance, the concept of "harm" (*ḍarar*) can be illustrated by a seller who promotes a product by convincing buyers of its high quality, when in reality the product lacks such quality. This deceitful transaction benefits the seller at the buyer's expense. An example of "to harm" (*ḍirār*) might involve a tree in one person's garden with branches extending into a neighbor's garden, causing leaves to fall into the neighbor's yard. Although the tree owner may have a limited gain from the tree, the neighbor is burdened with cleaning up the leaves. This demonstrates the importance of being considerate and ensuring one's actions do not inadvertently cause harm to others.

In other interpretations, "harm" (*ḍarar*) is understood as self-inflicted damage, while "to harm" (*ḍirār*) refers to causing harm to others.

Both interpretations are accurate, and supported by numerous Qur'anic verses and prophetic hadiths. Allah Almighty, advising people to respect the sanctity of the four sacred months, commands,

"فَلَا تَظْلِمُوا فِيهِنَّ أَنفُسَكُمْ"

"Do not wrong yourselves during them (the four sacred months) …"[167]

Similarly, the Prophet Muhammad (pbuh) stated in a hadith,

"الْمُسْلِمُ مَنْ سَلِمَ الْمُسْلِمُونَ مِنْ لِسَانِهِ وَيَدِهِ، وَالْمُهَاجِرُ مَنْ هَجَرَ مَا نَهَى اللَّهُ عَنْهُ"

[166] See Taftazani: *Sharh al-Taftazani 'ala al-Arba'in al-Nawawiyyah*, p. 196.

[167] Q. (9:36).

"A Muslim is the one who avoids harming Muslims with his tongue or his hands. And an emigrant *(muhajir)* is the one who gives up (abandons) all of what Allah has forbidden."[168]

The emphasis on the tongue first highlights the ease with which one can harm others through insults and lies, followed by the hand, acknowledging that its actions can have equally severe consequences.

[168] Shamsuddin al-Kirmani: *Al-Kawakib al-Darari fi Sharh Sahih al-Bukhari*, vol. 1, p. 88-9.

HADITH 33

الحديث الثالث والثلاثون

The Rights of the Plaintiff and the Accused

عَنْ ابْنِ عَبَّاسٍ رَضِيَ اللَّهُ عَنْهُمَا أَنَّ رَسُولَ اللَّهِ صَلَّى اللّهُ عَلَيْهِ وَسَلَّمَ قَالَ:
"لَوْ يُعْطَى النَّاسُ بِدَعْوَاهُمْ لَادَّعَى رِجَالٌ أَمْوَالَ قَوْمٍ وَدِمَاءَهُمْ، لَكِنَّ الْبَيِّنَةَ عَلَى الْمُدَّعِي، وَالْيَمِينَ عَلَى مَنْ أَنْكَرَ".
حَدِيثٌ حَسَنٌ، رَوَاهُ الْبَيْهَقِيّ، وَغَيْرُهُ هَكَذَا، وَبَعْضُهُ فِي الصَّحِيحَيْنِ.

On the authority of Ibn ʿAbbās (r.a.), that the Messenger of Allah (pbuh) said,

"Were people to be given everything that they claimed, men would (unjustly) claim the wealth and lives of (other) people. But, the onus of proof is upon the claimant, and the taking of an oath is upon him who denies."

Reliable hadith related by Al-Bayhaqī and others in this manner, and sections of the hadith are in *Ṣaḥīḥ al-Bukhārī* and *Ṣaḥīḥ Muslim*.

Theme

- The importance of law and justice in Islam

Explanation

This hadith underscores that Islam values not only worship and an individual's spiritual relationship with the Creator but also the protection and enforcement of law within society.

The Messenger of Allah (pbuh) highlights that without the presence and implementation of law, people would easily steal from others. Injustice and the absence of law lead to violence and chaos. The Prophet Muhammad (pbuh) was among the prophets who successfully led their societies based on Divine Teachings, which included the application of justice.

Scholars of Islamic jurisprudence have provided various interpretations of the terms "plaintiff" (*muddaʿī*) and "defendant." Some define the plaintiff as the one who initiates the legal process and is not required to swear an oath, while the defendant must swear an oath. However, the plaintiff must substantiate their claim with evidence.[169] For instance, if someone finds an unclaimed item, the plaintiff, or the rightful owner seeking its return, must prove their claim with evidence, whereas the defendant need only swear an oath.

Following the Prophetic example, Islamic leaders throughout history have prioritized law and its enforcement. This emphasis has fostered the development of Islamic civilization in Muslim regions such as Andalusia, Baghdad, and the Ottoman Empire. These societies produced scholars in various fields who laid the foundations for many sciences, benefiting the entire world to this day. It is also noteworthy that the first detailed book on international law was written by the Islamic scholar from Iraq, Muḥammad Shaybānī (d. 189/805), titled *The Islamic Law of Nations* (published in English by Johns Hopkins University Press).

[169] See Zayn al-Din ibn Shihab al-Din: *Jami' al-'Ulum wa al-Hikam*, p. 687.

HADITH 34

الحديث الرابع والثلاثون

Methods for Changing Evil

عَنْ أَبِي سَعِيدٍ الْخُدْرِيّ رَضِي اللهُ عَنْهُ قالَ: سَمِعتُ رسولَ اللهِ صَلَّى اللهُ عَلَيْهِ وَسَلَّمَ يقولُ:

"مَنْ رَأَى مِنْكُمْ مُنْكَرًا فَلْيُغَيِّرْهُ بِيَدِهِ، فَإِنْ لَمْ يَسْتَطِعْ فَبِلِسَانِهِ، فَإِنْ لَمْ يَسْتَطِعْ فَبِقَلْبِهِ، وَذَلِكَ أَضْعَفُ الْإِيمَانِ".

رَوَاهُ مُسْلِمٌ.

On the authority of Abū Sa'īd al-Khuḍrī (r.a.) who said: I heard the Messenger of Allah (pbuh) say,

"Whosoever of you sees an evil, let him change it with his hand; and if he is not able to do so, then (let him change it) with his tongue; and if he is not able to do so, then with his heart — and that is the weakest of faith."

Related by Muslim.

Theme

- Ways to prevent evil

Explanation

Islam is a faith that places special emphasis on "commanding good" and "forbidding evil," as Allah has commanded believers to be among those who advocate for good deeds and discourage wrongdoing. In the Qur'an, Allah has also described the Muslim community as the best community brought forth for humanity because they command what is right, forbid what is wrong, and believe in Allah.[170]

The hadith emphasizes that when a believer witnesses wrongdoing or immorality in society, they are obliged to take action based on their ability. If they can physically remove or change the evil, they must do so. If they cannot, the Messenger of Allah (pbuh) advises them to use their words to address it.

In today's world, opinions, analyses, and criticisms can be disseminated through various media, including the Internet, television, radio, and magazines. It is now possible for people on one continent to be informed about events on another within seconds. Despite technological advancements, evil deeds and immorality seem more prevalent than ever. Social vices once strictly prohibited are now not only legal in many countries but also encouraged by some social groups. Even though these vices—such as adultery, immorality, injustice, and other unethical behavior—are not encouraged, they are often accepted as a normal part of life in many societies.

Believers are thus tasked with using multiple platforms to reduce the spread of evil, fulfilling Prophet Muhammad's (pbuh) advice to prevent or change evil with their words. One prophetic teaching states that speaking the truth before a tyrant ruler is the highest form of jihad, underscoring the importance of vocal opposition to wrongdoing and immorality.[171]

In cases where a believer cannot change the evil with their hands or words, their heart should not be at ease when witnessing wrongdoing in society. There are instances where believers are threatened with their lives

---

[170] See Q. (3:104).

[171] See Abu Abdallah Muhammad ibn Yazid ibn Majah al-Qazwini: *Sunan ibn Majah*, Dar al-Risalah al-'Alamiyyah, Damascus, 2009, vol. 5, p. 144.

if they try to speak the truth or prevent evil. In such cases, their silence and inner rejection of the witnessed evil are sufficient.

Even though the Messenger of Allah (pbuh) advises preventing or changing evil through various methods, a believer should not actively seek out the faults or immoralities of others. Spying on others is forbidden.[172] Furthermore, according to Imam Aḥmad ibn Ḥanbal, the approach towards others should not be aggressive. Imam Aḥmad recounts that when the followers of the companion ʿAbdullāh ibn Mas ʿūd encountered people committing evil deeds, they would gently say, "Slow down, may Allah have mercy on you! Slow down, may Allah have mercy on you!" This was to encourage a more compassionate and non-confrontational approach.[173]

Those who strive to prevent evil should embody the following qualities: knowledge, avoidance of prohibitions, good manners, and compassion. The wrong act they are addressing should be clearly recognized as such, done openly, without spying, and occurring at that moment.

---

172 See the sayings of the classical Islamic scholar, Sufyan al-Thawri, and the renowned Islamic judge, Abu Ya'la, which are mentioned by Zayn al-Din ibn Shihab al-Din: *Jami' al-'Ulum wa al-Hikam*, p. 707-8.

173 Ibid.

HADITH 35

الحديث الخامس والثلاثون

The Sanctity of the Believer

عَنْ أَبِي هُرَيْرَةَ رَضِيَ اللهُ عَنْهُ قال: قالَ رسولُ اللهِ صَلَّى اللهُ عَلَيْهِ وَسَلَّمَ: "لَا تَحَاسَدُوا، وَلَا تَنَاجَشُوا، وَلَا تَبَاغَضُوا، وَلَا تَدَابَرُوا، وَلَا يَبِعْ بَعْضُكُمْ عَلَى بَيْعِ بَعْضٍ، وَكُونُوا عِبَادَ اللَّهِ إِخْوَانًا، الْمُسْلِمُ أَخُو الْمُسْلِمِ، لَا يَظْلِمُهُ، وَلَا يَخْذُلُهُ، وَلَا يَكْذِبُهُ، وَلَا يَحْقِرُهُ، التَّقْوَى هَاهُنَا، وَيُشِيرُ إِلَى صَدْرِهِ ثَلَاثَ مَرَّاتٍ، بِحَسْبِ امْرِئٍ مِنْ الشَّرِّ أَنْ يَحْقِرَ أَخَاهُ الْمُسْلِمَ، كُلُّ الْمُسْلِمِ عَلَى الْمُسْلِمِ حَرَامٌ: دَمُهُ وَمَالُهُ وَعِرْضُهُ".

رَوَاهُ مُسْلِمٌ.

On the authority of Abū Hurayrah (r.a.) who said:

The Messenger of Allah (pbuh) said, "Do not envy one another, and do not inflate prices for one another, and do not hate one another, and do not turn away from one another, and do not undercut one another in trade, but (rather) be slaves of Allah and brothers. A Muslim is the brother of a Muslim: he does not oppress him, nor does he fail him, nor does he lie to him, nor does he hold him in contempt. Piety (*taqwā*) is right here (and he pointed to his chest three times). It is evil enough for a man to hold his brother Muslim in contempt. The whole of a Muslim is inviolable for another Muslim: his blood, his property, and his honor."

Related by Muslim.

Theme

- The respectful behavior a Muslim should have towards another Muslim

Explanation

This hadith offers various pieces of advice and guidelines for believers to live harmoniously with one another. Adhering to these divine instructions not only preserves peace and brotherhood among believers but also earns the favor of Allah and His Messenger.

Envy (*ḥasad*) is the first sin manifested by Satan towards the first human, Adam (pbuh). When Satan was asked why he refused to bow to Adam (pbuh), even though he, along with the angels, was commanded by Allah to do so, he replied,

"قَالَ أَنَا خَيْرٌ مِّنْهُ خَلَقْتَنِي مِن نَّارٍ وَخَلَقْتَهُ مِن طِينٍ"

"I am better than him. You created me from fire, while You created him from clay."[174]

Satan (*Iblīs*) exhibited arrogance, which stemmed from his jealousy towards Adam (pbuh) when Allah commanded him and the angels to bow to Adam (pbuh). This attitude led to his downfall and punishment from Allah Almighty. Those who harbor envy and consider themselves superior to others will face the same consequences from the Lord of the Universe.

Not all individuals who experience jealousy will be held accountable on the Day of Judgment. Accountability will be for those who, due to envy, intend or act to harm others. In his work *Jāmiʿ al-ʿUlūm wa al-Ḥikam*, Imam Ibn Rajab discusses different types of people in relation to envy. Firstly, he mentions those who harbor envy internally without expressing it, and they are not judged by Allah for this. Secondly, he refers to those

---

[174] Q. (7:12).

who harbor envy and outwardly manifest it, causing harm to others; these individuals bear responsibility for this sin. Lastly, he mentions believers who strive to attain similar blessings for themselves as they observe in others, without desiring harm to them.[175]

The remedy for envy is found in gratitude towards Allah for everything He bestows and withholds. It is also found in accepting His decree with contentment. A person who sincerely appreciates their Creator will find their blessings augmented by Allah. In such a state, they do not covet what others possess. Allah promises increased blessings to those who show gratitude. The Qur'an states,

"وَإِذْ تَأَذَّنَ رَبُّكُمْ لَئِن شَكَرْتُمْ لَأَزِيدَنَّكُمْ وَلَئِن كَفَرْتُمْ إِنَّ عَذَابِي لَشَدِيدٌ"

"And (remember) when your Lord proclaimed: 'If you are grateful, I will certainly give you more; but if you are ungrateful, My punishment is severe.'"[176]

The Prophet Muhammad (pbuh) also warns against deceit in trade (*al-najsh*). Islamic scholars interpret *al-najsh* in two ways. According to Imam Ibn Rajab, the first category includes those who manipulate auction prices by artificially inflating them, not intending to purchase the goods, but rather to benefit the seller by raising prices or to harm the buyer.[177] Other scholars define it more broadly as any form of dishonesty or deception in commercial transactions.

---

175 Zayn al-Din ibn Shihab al-Din: *Jami' al-'Ulum wa al-Hikam*, p. 712.
176 Q. (14:7).
177 Zayn al-Din ibn Shihab al-Din: *Jami' al-'Ulum wa al-Hikam*, p. 714.

HADITH 36

الحديث السادس والثلاثون

Helping the Needy, Pursuing Knowledge, Reciting the Qur'an, and Rewards for Good Deeds

عَنْ أَبِي هُرَيْرَةَ رَضِيَ اللهُ عَنْهُ عَنْ النَّبِيِّ صَلَّى اللهُ عَلَيْهِ وَسَلَّمَ قَالَ:
"مَنْ نَفَّسَ عَنْ مُؤْمِنٍ كُرْبَةً مِنْ كُرَبِ الدُّنْيَا نَفَّسَ اللَّهُ عَنْهُ كُرْبَةً مِنْ كُرَبِ يَوْمِ الْقِيَامَةِ، وَمَنْ يَسَّرَ عَلَى مُعْسِرٍ، يَسَّرَ اللَّهُ عَلَيْهِ فِي الدُّنْيَا وَالْآخِرَةِ، وَمَنْ سَتَرَ مُسْلِما سَتَرَهُ اللهُ فِي الدُّنْيَا وَالْآخِرَةِ ، وَاللَّهُ فِي عَوْنِ الْعَبْدِ مَا كَانَ الْعَبْدُ فِي عَوْنِ أَخِيهِ، وَمَنْ سَلَكَ طَرِيقًا يَلْتَمِسُ فِيهِ عِلْمًا سَهَّلَ اللَّهُ لَهُ بِهِ طَرِيقًا إلَى الْجَنَّةِ، وَمَا اجْتَمَعَ قَوْمٌ فِي بَيْتٍ مِنْ بُيُوتِ اللَّهِ يَتْلُونَ كِتَابَ اللَّهِ، وَيَتَدَارَسُونَهُ فِيمَا بَيْنَهُمْ؛ إلَّا نَزَلَتْ عَلَيْهِمْ السَّكِينَةُ، وَغَشِيَتْهُمْ الرَّحْمَةُ، وَذَكَرَهُمْ اللَّهُ فِيمَنْ عِنْدَهُ، وَمَنْ أَبْطَأَ بِهِ عَمَلُهُ لَمْ يُسْرِعْ بِهِ نَسَبُهُ".

رَوَاهُ مُسْلِمٌ بهذا اللفظ.

On the authority of Abū Hurayrah (r.a.), that the Prophet (pbuh) said,

"Whoever removes a worldly grief from a believer, Allah will remove from him one of the griefs of the Day of Resurrection. And whoever alleviates the need of a needy person, Allah will alleviate his needs in this world and the Hereafter. Whoever shields (or hides the misdeeds of) a Muslim, Allah will shield him in this world and the Hereafter. And Allah will aid His slave so long as he aids his brother. And whoever follows a path to seek knowledge therein, Allah will make easy for him a path to Paradise. No people gather together in one of the Houses of Allah, reciting the Book of Allah and studying it among themselves, except that tranquility descends upon them, and mercy envelops them, and the angels surround them, and Allah mentions them amongst those who are with Him. And whoever is slowed down by his actions, will not be hastened forward by his lineage."

Related by Muslim with this wording

Themes

- The benefits bestowed by God when one helps another
- Acquiring Islamic knowledge paves the way to paradise
- Blessings derived from reading the Qur'an
- Lineage does not benefit a person in the scale of deeds on the Day of Judgment

Explanation

As emphasized in several earlier hadiths, this hadith underscores the significance of aiding others and the duty of believers to support those in need. Acts of compassion are directly linked to divine assistance and the mercy bestowed upon believers who engage in such deeds.

No matter how significant the kindness shown by a believer towards another person, it is incomparable to the blessings they receive from God in this world and the Hereafter. For instance, alleviating someone's sorrow may take very little time, whereas preventing suffering that could last for centuries in the Hereafter is far more valuable and important.

Anas bin Mālik (r.a.) narrates a hadith from the Messenger of Allah (pbuh), emphasizing the importance of kindness to others:

"عَنْ أَنَسِ بْنِ مَالِكٍ، أَنّ النَّبِيَّ صَلَّى اللَّهُ عَلَيْهِ وَسَلَّمَ قَالَ: "الْخَلْقُ كُلُّهُمْ عِيَالُ اللَّهِ، فَأَحَبُّ الْخَلْقِ إِلَى اللَّهِ أَنْفَعُهُمْ لِعِيَالِهِ".

"All of humanity is Allah's creation, and the most beloved to Allah is the one who is most beneficial to His creation."[178]

The initial hadith also underscores the importance of seeking knowledge. The Prophet (pbuh) placed great emphasis on acquiring knowledge, associating it with the path to Paradise. Knowledge is a profound blessing, benefiting a person not only in the Hereafter but also in this world. Possessing knowledge unlocks many other blessings in this life. In the Qur'an, Allah the Almighty highlights that He bestowed wealth and vast dominion upon Prophet David (pbuh) and Prophet Solomon (pbuh), but foremost, He mentions the blessing of knowledge before all other blessings:

"وَلَقَدْ آتَيْنَا دَاوُودَ وَسُلَيْمَانَ عِلْمًا وَقَالاَ الْحَمْدُ لِلَّهِ الَّذِي فَضَّلَنَا عَلَى كَثِيرٍ مِّنْ عِبَادِهِ الْمُؤْمِنِينَ. وَوَرِثَ سُلَيْمَانُ دَاوُودَ وَقَالَ يَا أَيُّهَا النَّاسُ عُلِّمْنَا مَنطِقَ الطَّيْرِ وَأُوتِينَا مِن كُلِّ شَيْءٍ إِنَّ هَذَا لَهُوَ الْفَضْلُ الْمُبِينُ. وَحُشِرَ لِسُلَيْمَانَ جُنُودُهُ مِنَ الْجِنِّ وَالْإِنسِ وَالطَّيْرِ فَهُمْ يُوزَعُونَ".

"We gave knowledge to David and Solomon, and they said, 'Praise be to Allah, who has favored us over many of His believing servants!' Solomon inherited David. He said, 'O people, we have been taught the speech of birds and have been given from all things. Indeed, this is a clear favor.' Before Solomon, his army of jinn, men, and birds were gathered, and they were marching in rows."[179]

Above all, knowledge should be acquired in a manner that benefits both the seeker and humanity, without causing harm. Furthermore, it should be such that it brings a person closer to the Creator. In fact, a proper understanding of the Creator is the essence of all knowledge. One cannot truly know their Creator without learning about His qualities and attributes, nor can one easily believe in the Hereafter without the correct

---

178 al-Bayhaqi: *Al-Jami' li Shu'ab al-Iman*, vol. 9, p. 523.

179 Q. (27:15-7).

concept of it. The knowledge of God is so fundamental in Islam that it precedes even the declaration of faith. The Qur'an states,

"فَاعْلَمْ أَنَّهُ لَا إِلَٰهَ إِلَّا اللَّهُ"

"So know, that there is no deity except Allah."[180]

Therefore, a person must first attain a certain level of knowledge to understand that there is no true god but Allah, and then reach the level of firm belief. The deeper one's knowledge about something, the better one can perceive and understand it. Our Creator has designed human nature in such a way that gaining a clear perception of things enables a person to distinguish between good and evil. The more knowledge they acquire about evils, the more they can avoid them; conversely, the more knowledge they have about good, the more they value and strive to practice or benefit from it. ʿUmar (r.a.) famously said that he learned about evils not to fall into them but to prevent himself from doing so, adding that those who lack knowledge of evil are likely to fall into it.

Beneficial knowledge about God's creation, including the sciences related to the laws of nature, is not only permissible in Islam but also encouraged to be explored.

Throughout the centuries, many have drawn a dividing line between the natural sciences and Islamic sciences. However, it was Muslim scholars who laid the foundations and made significant contributions to various fields such as algebra, geometry, medicine, and international law. They invented the clock and the solar measurement system to ensure timely prayers, and established sophisticated water canalization systems in Muslim cities during an era when European cities were plagued by unsanitary conditions and viruses, the sources of epidemics. These advancements were driven by the Islamic requirement for physical cleanliness before prayers and after intimate relations.

People are encouraged to study natural sciences to gain a deeper understanding of their Creator and to serve Him. The Qur'an and the

---

[180] Q. (47:19).

hadiths of Prophet Muhammad (pbuh) served as primary sources of inspiration for many Muslim scholars, who initially specialized in Islamic disciplines before branching into the exact and natural sciences. Here are some Qur'anic verses requesting people to ponder:

"إِنَّ فِي خَلْقِ السَّمَاوَاتِ وَالْأَرْضِ وَاخْتِلَافِ اللَّيْلِ وَالنَّهَارِ لَآيَاتٍ لِأُولِي الْأَلْبَابِ. الَّذِينَ يَذْكُرُونَ اللَّهَ قِيَامًا وَقُعُودًا وَعَلَى جُنُوبِهِمْ وَيَتَفَكَّرُونَ فِي خَلْقِ السَّمَاوَاتِ وَالْأَرْضِ رَبَّنَا مَا خَلَقْتَ هَذَا بَاطِلًا سُبْحَانَكَ فَقِنَا عَذَابَ النَّارِ"

"Indeed, in the creation of the heavens and the earth and the alternation of the night and the day are signs for those of understanding. Those who remember Allah while standing, sitting, and lying on their sides and give thought to the creation of the heavens and the earth, (saying), 'Our Lord, You did not create this aimlessly; exalted are You (above such a thing); then protect us from the punishment of the Fire.'"[181]

It is also mentioned,

"أَوَلَمْ يَرَ الَّذِينَ كَفَرُوا أَنَّ السَّمَاوَاتِ وَالْأَرْضَ كَانَتَا رَتْقًا فَفَتَقْنَاهُمَا وَجَعَلْنَا مِنَ الْمَاءِ كُلَّ شَيْءٍ حَيٍّ أَفَلَا يُؤْمِنُونَ"

"Have those who disbelieved not considered that the heavens and the earth were a joined entity, and We separated them and made from water every living thing? Then will they not believe?"[182]

The study of Islamic sciences should be pursued with pure sincerity, good intentions, and adherence to permissible matters. It is narrated that Imam 'Abdullāh ibn Idrīs al-Shāfi'ī (d. 204/820) once struggled with memorizing Qur'anic verses after encountering something not appropriate to look at. He shared this experience in a poem:

---

[181] Q. (3:190-1).

[182] Q. (21:30).

شكوت إلى وكيع سوء حفظي فأرشدني إلى ترك المعاص

وقال اعلم بأن العلم فضل وفضل الله لا يؤتاه عاصي

"I complained to (my teacher) Wakīʿ about my difficulty in memorization,

He guided me to abandon sins and said,

'Know that knowledge is a favor,

And the favor of Allah is not given to a sinner.'"[183]

Knowledge, despite its countless benefits, cannot alone guide a person to the Creator; rather, it marks the initial step in the journey towards Him. Subsequently, believers draw closer to the Creator and ascend spiritually through various endeavors. This journey commences with refraining from the forbidden, followed by earnest efforts.

In this hadith, the benefits that come from Allah for those who read and learn the Qur'an in His houses (mosques) are highlighted, though they are not limited to these settings. Among the benefits mentioned is spiritual tranquility, which provides a sense of security during the various challenges life presents.

Reading the Qur'an is recommended in several Qur'anic verses and numerous hadiths of Prophet Muhammad (pbuh), as is reflecting upon its verses. The specific Islamic science of Qur'anic Exegesis (*tafsīr*) is regarded as the most important among the Islamic sciences. At the beginning of his Qur'anic exegesis, Al-Baḥr al-Madīd fī Tafsīr al-Qur'ān al-Majīd, the scholar Aḥmad ibn ʿAjībah al-Ḥasanī (d. 1224/1808) introduces his work by praising Allah and invoking blessings upon Prophet Muhammad (pbuh), stating, "The science of exegesis (*tafsīr*) of the Qur'an is the most exalted of all sciences, the most beneficial, influencing the ultimate development of ideas and the refinement of meanings."

183 Muhammad ibn Abi Bakr, known as Ibn al-Qayyim al-Jawziyyah: *Al-Jawab al-Kafi liman sa'ala 'an al-Dawa' al-Shafi*, Dar al-Ma'rifah, Beirut, 1997, p. 52.

Among the various benefits, Allah's mercy towards humanity is also mentioned. Mercy signifies forgiveness, love, compassion, and care. It is Allah's mercy that becomes the primary reason for a person's entry into paradise. Therefore, the believer, by reading the Qur'an, learning it, and living by its verses, paves his way to paradise.

The Messenger of Allah (pbuh) also mentions that angels surround the believer who reads and learns the Qur'an. This angelic presence signifies protection from evils. Allah sends His angels to safeguard those who engage with the Qur'an.

Another benefit mentioned in this hadith is the honor Allah bestows upon those who read and learn the Qur'an by mentioning them in the company of His close servants. This is a significant recognition. If being praised and remembered positively by others in this world brings a special spiritual joy, love, and trust, it encourages righteous actions. Maintaining a good reputation in this world is important, but how much more important and valuable is the same reputation in the Hereafter? This reputation is eternal and not subject to the fleeting opinions of this world. It includes the esteemed views of those close to Allah—prophets, angels, the sincere, martyrs, and His devout servants.

At the end of the hadith, the Messenger of Allah (pbuh) clearly states that a person will not benefit from his relatives if there are deficiencies in his own record of deeds. Each individual is responsible for their actions. The Prophet (pbuh) emphasizes this because it is common for people to boast or rely on the status of their authoritative, wealthy, or powerful relatives.

HADITH 37

الحديث السابع والثلاثون

The Gifts and Mercy of Allah

عَنْ ابْنِ عَبَّاسٍ رَضِيَ اللَّهُ عَنْهُمَا عَنْ رَسُولِ اللَّهِ صَلَّى اللهُ عَلَيْهِ وَسَلَّمَ فِيمَا يَرْوِيهِ عَنْ رَبِّهِ تَبَارَكَ وَتَعَالَى، قَالَ:

"إِنَّ اللَّهَ كَتَبَ الْحَسَنَاتِ وَالسَّيِّئَاتِ، ثُمَّ بَيَّنَ ذَلِكَ، فَمَنْ هَمَّ بِحَسَنَةٍ فَلَمْ يَعْمَلْهَا كَتَبَهَا اللَّهُ عِنْدَهُ حَسَنَةً كَامِلَةً، وَإِنْ هَمَّ بِهَا فَعَمِلَهَا كَتَبَهَا اللَّهُ عِنْدَهُ عَشْرَ حَسَنَاتٍ إِلَى سَبْعِمِائَةِ ضِعْفٍ إِلَى أَضْعَافٍ كَثِيرَةٍ، وَإِنْ هَمَّ بِسَيِّئَةٍ فَلَمْ يَعْمَلْهَا كَتَبَهَا اللَّهُ عِنْدَهُ حَسَنَةً كَامِلَةً، وَإِنْ هَمَّ بِهَا فَعَمِلَهَا كَتَبَهَا اللَّهُ سَيِّئَةً وَاحِدَةً".

رَوَاهُ الْبُخَارِيُّ وَمُسْلِمٌ فِي صَحِيحَيْهِمَا بِهَذِهِ الْحُرُوفِ.

"From Ibn ʿAbbās (r.a.), from the Messenger of Allah (pbuh), from that which he narrates from His Lord, the Blessed and Exalted, that He said,

"Allah has written down the good deeds and the bad deeds." Then he explained it (by saying that), "He who considered doing a good deed and has not done it, Allah writes it down with Himself as a full good deed, but if he considered doing it and has done it, Allah writes it down with Himself as from ten good deeds to seven hundred times, or many times over. But if he considered doing a bad deed and has not done it, Allah writes it down with Himself as a full good deed, but if he considered doing it and has done it, Allah writes it down as one bad deed."

Related by al-Bukhārī and Muslim in their authentic compilations with the exact texts.

Theme

- Facilitating the attainment of multiplied rewards

Explanation

At the outset of this hadith, the Lord of the Universe declares, "Indeed, He has recorded the good and bad deeds, and then He has clarified them." These deeds are inscribed in the "Preserved Tablet" (*Lawḥ al-Maḥfūdh*), where the entire Qur'an was recorded before Archangel Gabriel conveyed it to Prophet Muhammad (pbuh). God's explanation of these deeds includes defining them and elucidating the consequences that arise from their enactment. The "Tablet" also contains undisclosed information about humanity.

Furthermore, Allah Almighty instructs us through the Prophet Muhammad (pbuh): "Whoever intends to perform a good deed but does not carry it out, Allah records it for them as if they had completed it." This exemplifies one of God's concessions to believers. However, this ruling does not apply if a person fails due to obstacles or similar reasons; rather, it applies when the deed is genuinely impossible to perform.

Continuing, the hadith states, "And if one intends to perform a good deed and completes it, Allah records it for them ten to seven hundred times, and even more." Here, God expresses His desire for manifold rewards for humanity's acts of kindness. The phrase "and even more" indicates the potential for limitless rewards from God towards His creation.

According to Imam Taftāzāni, for a good deed to yield substantial rewards, sincerity, adherence to conditions and rules of righteous conduct, and its amplification must all be considered.[184]

In the concluding part of the hadith, the consequences of contemplating or committing an evil deed are outlined, stating: "If one intends to commit

---

184 See the explanation of Sa'd al-Din Masud bin Umar bin Abd Allah: *Sharh al-Taftazani ala al-Arbain al-Nawawiyyah*, p. 213.

an evil deed but refrains, Allah records it as a complete good deed." This segment of the hadith illustrates God's mercy towards His creation. He is willing to pardon and reward the believer simply for abstaining from wrongdoing. It's crucial to understand that this forgiveness isn't due to an inability to commit the sin but stems from a conscious decision not to do so, driven by a moral Islamic principle or fear of God. Such a believer merits a reward from Allah.

Conversely, if someone intends and commits an evil deed, God records only one transgression for them. This reflects God's justice towards humanity, demonstrating His preference for rewarding rather than punishing, facilitated through various means.

It is also affirmed that good deeds and intentions, which carry significant weight and reward with the Lord, are multiplied because they originate from the heart of man, inspired by Divine guidance. In contrast, evil deeds stem from human whims and the influence of the accursed devil, holding no weight with God. However, it's important to note that the evil actions mentioned in this hadith pertain to deeds that do not harm others or become habitual practices. Otherwise, the person who initiates such actions bears the sins of all who follow suit, as narrated by Mundhir ibn Jarīr from his father, who heard the Messenger of Allah say,

"وَمَنْ سَنَّ فِي الْإِسْلَامِ سُنَّةً سَيِّئَةً كَانَ عَلَيْهِ وِزْرُهَا وَوِزْرُ مَنْ عَمِلَ بِهَا مِنْ بَعْدِهِ مِنْ غَيْرِ أَنْ يَنْقُصَ مِنْ أَوْزَارِهِمْ شَيْءٌ"

"Whoever introduces a bad practice (*sunnah sayyiah*) in Islam, bears its sin and the sins of all those who act upon it afterward, without diminishing their own sins in the least."[185]

---

[185] Muslim ibn al-Haj-jaj: *Sahih Muslim*, vol. 1, p. 452.

HADITH 38

الحديث الثامن والثلاثون

Drawing Closer to Allah

عَنْ أَبِي هُرَيْرَة قَالَ: قَالَ رَسُول اللَّهِ إنَّ اللَّهَ تَعَالَى قَالَ:
"مَنْ عَادَى لِي وَلِيًّا فَقْد آذَنْتهُ بِالْحَرْبِ، وَمَا تَقَرَّبَ إلَيَّ عَبْدِي بِشَيْءٍ أَحَبَّ إلَيَّ مِمَّا افْتَرَضْتُهُ عَلَيْهِ، وَلَا يَزَالُ عَبْدِي يَتَقَرَّبُ إلَيَّ بِالنَّوَافِلِ حَتَّى أُحِبَّهُ، فَإِذَا أَحْبَبْتُهُ كُنْت سَمْعَهُ الَّذِي يَسْمَعُ بِهِ، وَبَصَرَهُ الَّذِي يُبْصِرُ بِهِ، وَيَدَهُ الَّتِي يَبْطِشُ بِهَا، وَرِجْلَهُ الَّتِي يَمْشِي بِهَا، وَلَئِنْ سَأَلَنِي لَأُعْطِيَنَّهُ، وَلَئِنْ اسْتَعَاذَنِي لَأُعِيذَنَّهُ".
رَوَاهُ الْبُخَارِيّ.

On the authority of Abū Hurayrah (r.a.) who said,

The Messenger of Allah (pbuh) said, "Verily Allah the Almighty said: 'Whosoever shows enmity to a friend (*waliyy*) of Mine, then I have declared war against him. And My servant does not draw near to Me with anything more loved to Me than the religious duties I have obligated upon him. And My servant continues to draw near to me with supererogatory (*nāfilah)* deeds until I Love him. When I Love him, I am his hearing with which he hears, and his sight with which he sees, and his hand with which he strikes, and his foot with which he walks. Were he to ask (something) of Me, I would surely give it to him; and were he to seek refuge with Me, I would surely grant him refuge."

Related by al-Bukhārī.

Themes

- Definition and qualities of the "Friend of Allah" (*waliyy*)
- Consequences of hostility towards Allah's friends
- Drawing closer to Allah through good deeds

Explanation

The term "*waliyy*," originating from Arabic, encompasses several closely related meanings. In numerous Qur'anic verses and prophetic hadiths, it is defined as a friend, ally, protector, or close companion. The plural form of *waliyy* is *awliyā'*.

An essential question arises: What are the categories of the *awliyā'* and what qualities do they possess? In regards to the categories, the Qur'an states,

"إِنَّمَا وَلِيُّكُمُ ٱللَّهُ وَرَسُولُهُۥ وَٱلَّذِينَ ءَامَنُوا۟ ٱلَّذِينَ يُقِيمُونَ ٱلصَّلَوٰةَ وَيُؤْتُونَ ٱلزَّكَوٰةَ وَهُمْ رَٰكِعُونَ"

"Your allies are none but Allah and (therefore) His Messenger and those who have believed - those who establish prayer and give *zakāh*, and they bow (in worship)."[186]

The following hadith that is narrated by 'Umar bin al-Khaṭṭāb (r.a.) and recorded in Sunan Abū Dāwūd, describes the "friends of Allah," stating,

"إِنَّ مِنْ عِبَادِ اللَّهِ لأُنَاسًا مَا هُمْ بِأَنْبِيَاءَ وَلاَ شُهَدَاءَ يَغْبِطُهُمُ الأَنْبِيَاءُ وَالشُّهَدَاءُ يَوْمَ الْقِيَامَةِ بِمَكَانِهِمْ مِنَ اللَّهِ تَعَالَى." قَالُوا يَا رَسُولَ اللَّهِ تُخْبِرُنَا مَنْ هُمْ؟ قَالَ "هُمْ قَوْمٌ تَحَابُّوا بِرُوحِ اللَّهِ عَلَى غَيْرِ أَرْحَامٍ بَيْنَهُمْ وَلاَ أَمْوَالٍ يَتَعَاطَوْنَهَا فَوَاللَّهِ إِنَّ وُجُوهَهُمْ لَنُورٌ وَإِنَّهُمْ عَلَى نُورٍ لاَ يَخَافُونَ إِذَا خَافَ النَّاسُ وَلاَ يَحْزَنُونَ إِذَا حَزِنَ

---

[186] Q. (5:54).

النَّاسُ". وَقَرَأَ هَذِهِ الآيَةَ: "أَلاَ إِنَّ أَوْلِيَاءَ اللَّهِ لاَ خَوْفٌ عَلَيْهِمْ وَلاَ هُمْ يَحْزَنُونَ".

"Indeed, among the servants of Allah are some people who are neither prophets nor martyrs. The prophets and martyrs will envy them on the Day of Judgment for their rank before Allah." The Companions of the Prophet asked, "O Messenger of Allah, who are they?" He replied, "They are people who loved one another for the sake of Allah, without any kinship or financial interest. By Allah, their faces will radiate light, and they will be upon light. They will not fear when others fear, nor will they grieve when others grieve." Then he recited the Qur'anic verse, "Unquestionably, for the allies of Allah, there will be no fear concerning them, nor will they grieve."[187]

In *Al-Baḥr al-Madīd fī tafsīr al-Qurān al-Majīd*, Ibn ʿAjībah defines the *awliyā'* as those who demonstrate their friendship through submission to Allah (*al-ṭāʿah*) and to whom Allah shows His friendship through miracles. He further categorizes *awliyā'* among the believers into two groups:

1. The general category (*wilāyah al-ʿāmmah*), which includes all those who possess faith and devotion to Allah.
2. The special category (*wilāyah al-khāṣṣah*), which includes those who have attained deep knowledge of Allah, are immersed in His love (*ahl al-fanā'*), and await divine manifestations (*ahl al-baqā'*). These individuals blend Islamic jurisprudence (sharia) with divine reality (*ḥaqīqah*), are adorned with proper Islamic manners, completely detached from materialism, and possess complete love for Allah.[188]

Imam Al-Qushayrī, in his Qur'anic exegesis book, *Laṭāf al-Ishārāt*, describes the qualities of the *awliyā'*:

---

187 Q. (10:62) : Abu Dawud al-Sijistani: *Sunan Abi Dawud*, vol. 5, p. 387.

188 Ahmad ibn ʿAjībah al-Hasani: *El-Bahr al-Madid fi Tafsir al-Quran al-Majid*, vol. 3, p. 172.

"Every prophet is infallible (*maʿṣūm*) and every *waliyy* is protected (*maḥfūẓ*). The difference between 'protected' and 'infallible' is that the infallible one, despite possible shortcomings, is never affected by them, nor are they considered sinners. The protected one might have shortcomings considered as sins, but he does not persist in sinning."[189]

Imam then cites the Qur'anic verse that describes their qualities: "... those who, when they commit an immorality or wrong themselves (by transgression), remember Allah and seek forgiveness for their sins."[190]

Allah grants His friends (*awliyā'*) the ability to perform miracles, known as "*karāmāt*," which are a step below the miracles of the Prophets.[191] These miracles demonstrate the blessings Allah has granted them and testify to Allah's existence. Their qualities are further highlighted in the hadith being commented upon, where it is emphasized that Allah loves them, guides them on the straight Islamic path, protects them from many evils, and enables them to spread the blessings of Islam.

An important point in this hadith is that those who harm the *awliyā'* of Allah have declared war on Allah and are assured defeat. Scholars caution against harming or wronging anyone, as it is unknown who the *awliyā'* of Allah are, for only Allah knows the hearts of people. The esteemed Islamic scholar from the early generations of Muslims, Ḥasan al-Baṣri (d. 110/728), said,

"قَالَ الحَسَنُ بْنُ آدَمَ: هَلْ لَكَ بِمُحَارَبَةِ اللَّهِ مِنْ طَاقَةٍ؟ فَإِنَّ مَنْ عَصَى اللَّهَ فَقَدْ حَارَبَهُ، لَكِنْ كُلَّمَا كَانَ الذَّنْبُ أَقْبَحَ، كَانَ أَشَدَّ مُحَارَبَةً لِلَّهِ، وَلِهَذَا سَمَّى اللَّهُ تَعَالَى أَكَلَةَ الرِّبَا وَقُطَّاعَ الطَّرِيقِ مُحَارِبِينَ لِلَّهِ تَعَالَى وَرَسُولِهِ؛ لِعِظَمِ ظُلْمِهِمْ لِعِبَادِهِ، وَسَعْيِهِمْ بِالفَسَادِ فِي بِلَادِهِ، وَكَذَلِكَ مُعَادَاةُ أَوْلِيَائِهِ، فَإِنَّهُ تَعَالَى يَتَوَلَّى نُصْرَةَ

[189] Abu al-Qasim al-Qushayri: *Lataif al-Isharat*, Dar al-Kutub al-Ilmiyyah, Beirut, 2000, vol. 2, p. 22.

[190] Q. (4:17).

[191] See Kemal Hasan Mar'i: *Al-Majmu' al-Kabir min al-Mutun fima yudhkar min al-Funun*, Al-Maktabah al-Asriyyah, Beirut, 2005, vol. 1, p. 34.

أَوْلِيَائِهِ، وَيُحِبُّهُمْ وَيُؤَيِّدُهُمْ، فَمَنْ عَادَاهُمْ، فَقَدْ عَادَى اللَّهَ وَحَارَبَهُ".

"Do you think you have the strength to fight Allah? Anyone who opposes Allah is waging war against Him. The greater the sin, the greater the war declared against Allah. This is why Allah has called the taking of interest and cutting off pathways as two wars against Allah and His Messenger. This is due to the great injustice or oppression towards Allah's servants, destructive efforts on His lands, and enmity towards His *awliyā'*. Thus, Allah Almighty supports His *awliyā'*, loves and assists them. Whoever shows enmity towards them has shown enmity towards Allah and declared war on Him."[192]

The continuation of the hadith speaks about the closeness of the Creator with two categories of believers:

1. Those who fulfill obligatory religious duties and thereby draw nearer to Allah.
2. Those who, besides the obligatory duties, draw closer to their Creator through supererogatory acts, such as fasting on Mondays and Thursdays, reading the Qur'an outside of prayer, performing additional prayers beyond the obligatory ones, and more.

Believers who fulfill both categories become those whom Allah loves.

The word love (*ḥub*), mentioned in this hadith, has various definitions. In the book, *Al-Risālah al-Qushayriyyah*, Imam al-Qushayrī defines it in this way: "The bubbles that froth on the sea's surface from heavy rain are called *ḥubab*. Similarly, pure love (of a believer) bubbles in the heart when it thirsts and yearns for a swift meeting with the Beloved (Allah)."[193] This definition connects the origin of the word love in Arabic to the spiritual experience of the believer for their Creator.

Regarding Allah's love for His servant, Imam Al-Qushayrī describes it as Allah's desire to bestow blessings upon a specific believer. These blessings and rewards stem from His mercy. However, love is more special than

---

[192] Zayn al-Din ibn Shihab al-Din: *Jami' al-Ulum wa al-Hikam*, p. 774.

[193] Al-Qushayri: *Al-Risalah al-Qushayriyyah*, p. 520.

mercy. The desire to grant His servant closeness and high spiritual ranks is called love (*maḥabbah*).

Although Allah's love for His creation is immense, this hadith specifically discusses Allah's special love for the believer, manifested and reflected in the believer's heart. Allah's satisfaction and love for the believer is their ultimate achievement in this world. When the believer attains this, their heart is devoid of materialism, and the statement of Unity, "There is no god but Allah" (*Lā ilāha il-lā All-llāh*), becomes a reality, verified, and constantly mentioned in their heart. Being in continuous contact with divine reality, their body parts follow the heart, motivating good deeds and signaling other body parts to adhere to Allah's limits and work in His path. In this way, the believer becomes a manifestation of the "Divine Attributes" of Allah.

In the book, *Sharḥ al-Taftazānī ʿalā al-Arbaʿīn al-Nawawī*, the author quotes a saying by Imam Junayd al-Bagdādī (d. 297/910), stating that Allah's love for a person is manifested in the endowment of the attributes to the beloved (the believer) by the Beloved (Allah).[194]

Imam Abū Bakr Al-Kattānī (d. 322/934) narrates that during the time of Hajj, Imam Junayd was asked by the present scholars about love. He was the youngest in the group. After lowering his head and weeping, he replied,

Love is like a servant of Allah who abandons his desires and is devoted to the remembrance of Allah (*dhikr Allāh*). He remains steadfast in fulfilling religious obligations, being conscious of Allah's presence in his heart. The radiance of his essence ignites his heart. He partakes in the pure cup of His (Allah's) love. The Almighty reveals Himself to him beyond unseen veils.[195] Thus, when he speaks, he speaks from Allah, and everything he says is from Allah. When he moves, he moves by Allah's command. When he stands, he stands with Allah. He is for Allah, of Allah, and with Allah.

---

[194] Sa'd al-Din Masud bin Umar bin Abd Allah: *Sharh al-Taftazani ala al-Arba'in al-Nawawiyyah*, p. 219: It is important that the expression is not understood literally, but figuratively. The Imam does not intend to imply that the Divine Attributes become part of human nature, but rather that they serve as an exemplar.

[195] This revelation does not take a physical form, but is witnessed in the heart of the believer. The expression should not be taken in a physical sense, but in a spiritual one.

Upon hearing this, the scholars present wept, and one of them said, "No further explanation is needed. May Allah strengthen you, O crown of the gnostics (*tāj al-ʿārifīn*)!"[196]

The blessings that arise from divine love are numerous and perhaps countless. Numerous hadiths discuss these blessings extensively. Towards the end of this hadith, two of these blessings are mentioned: the acceptance of prayers and protection.

Additionally, in another hadith narrated by Abū Hurayrah (r.a.), the Messenger of Allah mentions another blessing where Allah exalts the believer He loves with these words:

"إِنَّ اللَّهَ إِذَا أَحَبَّ عَبْدًا دَعَا جِبْرِيلَ، فَقَالَ: إِنِّي أُحِبُّ فُلَانًا فَأَحِبَّهُ، قَالَ: فَيُحِبُّهُ جِبْرِيلُ، ثُمَّ يُنَادِي فِي السَّمَاءِ فَيَقُولُ: إِنَّ اللَّهَ يُحِبُّ فُلَانًا فَأَحِبُّوهُ، فَيُحِبُّهُ أَهْلُ السَّمَاءِ، قَالَ: ثُمَّ يُوضَعُ لَهُ الْقَبُولُ فِي الْأَرْضِ".

"If Allah loves a servant, He calls Gabriel and says, 'I love this person, so love him.' The Messenger of Allah said: "Then Gabriel loves him and announces in the heavens, 'Allah loves this person, so love him.' The inhabitants of the heavens then love him as well."[197]

One of the prayers of the Prophet (pbuh) that Imam Al-Tirmidhī reports was the following:

"اللَّهُمَّ إِنِّي أَسْأَلُكَ حُبَّكَ وَحُبَّ مَنْ يُحِبُّكَ وَالْعَمَلَ الَّذِي يُبَلِّغُنِي حُبَّكَ اللَّهُمَّ اجْعَلْ حُبَّكَ أَحَبَّ إِلَيَّ مِنْ نَفْسِي وَمَالِي وَأَهْلِي وَمِنَ الْمَاءِ الْبَارِدِ"

"O God, I ask You for Your love, the love of those who love You, and deeds which will cause me to attain Your love. O God, make Your love dearer to me than myself, my property, my family, and the cold water."[198]

---

[196] Al-Qushayrī: *Al-Risalah al-Qushayriyyah*, p. 528.

[197] Muslim ibn al-Hajjaj: *Sahih Muslim*, vol. 2, p. 1217.

[198] Muhammad ibn Isa al-Tirmidhi: *Shama'il al-Nabiyy*, vol. 5, p. 522-3.

HADITH 39

الحديث التاسع والثلاثون

Facilitation in the Face of Forgetfulness

عَنِ ابنِ عبَّاسٍ رَضِيَ اللهُ عَنْهُما، أَنَّ رسولَ اللهِ صَلَّى اللهُ عَلَيْهِ وَسَلَّمَ قالَ:
"إنَّ اللهَ تَجَاوَزَ لِي عَنْ أُمَّتِي: الْخَطَأَ، وَالنِّسْيَانَ، وَمَا اسْتُكْرِهُوا عَلَيْهِ".
حديثٌ حسَنٌ رواه ابنُ ماجَه والبيهقيُّ وغيرُهما.

On the authority of Ibn ʿAbbas (r.a.), that the Messenger of Allah (pbuh) said,

"Verily Allah has pardoned (or been lenient with) for me my ummah: their mistakes, their forgetfulness, and that which they have been forced to do under duress."

A reliable (*ḥasan*) hadith related by Ibn Mājah, and al-Bayhaqī and others.

Theme

- Divine justice and the simplification of the reckoning of human deeds by the Almighty

Explanation

One of God's immense blessings upon humanity is His merciful approach in not judging His creation for actions committed unintentionally, out of forgetfulness, or under compulsion.

Regarding the term "mistake" (*al-khaṭa'*), Islamic scholars have clarified that *al-khaṭa'* encompasses performing a wrongful act unintentionally. Moreover, scholars and judges who exert their efforts (*ijtihād*) in researching a matter and err unintentionally are still rewarded by God, as their intentions were sincere, and they utilized all their capacities.[199] The Prophet of Allah (pbuh) stated,

"إِذَا حَكَمَ الحَاكِمُ، فَاجْتَهَدَ، ثُمَّ أَصَابَ، فَلَهُ أَجْرَانِ، وَإِنْ حَكَمَ وَاجْتَهَدَ، فَأَخْطَأَ، فَلَهُ أَجْرٌ".

"When a judge makes an effort (*ijtihād*) and reaches the correct conclusion, he receives two rewards (from God). But if he makes an effort and errs, he receives one reward (from God)."[200]

The main hadith also addresses forgetfulness, a common human frailty. Imam Taftāzānī mentions that forgetfulness is categorized into two types:

1. Excusable forgetfulness
2. Inexcusable forgetfulness.

Excusable forgetfulness occurs when a person forgets to perform an act and does not remember it later. For example, someone might pray three prayer units (*rak'ah)* thinking they have prayed four. This type of forgetfulness is excusable.

In contrast, inexcusable forgetfulness happens when someone prays three *rak'ah* thinking they have prayed four, but then remembers. They are obliged to complete the four *rak'ah* once they recall. Thus, an act performed in forgetfulness cannot be deemed complete without correction or repetition once the person remembers.

The hadith's final part mentions that Allah forgives bad actions performed under compulsion. An example is someone in a situation

---

[199] See Sa'd al-Din Masud bin Umar bin Abd Allah: *Sharh al-Taftazani ala al-Arba'in al-Nawawiyyah*, p. 225.

[200] Muslim ibn al-Hajjaj: *Sahih Muslim*, vol. 2, p. 821.

where no food is available except that which is forbidden in Islam. In such a case, they are allowed to consume enough to survive, as preserving life is paramount.

Another example is a believer facing execution for their pure Islamic beliefs; denying these beliefs to save their life is permitted as long as the denial is not from the heart. Allah says in the Qur'an,

"مَن كَفَرَ بِاللَّهِ مِن بَعْدِ إِيمَانِهِ إِلَّا مَنْ أُكْرِهَ وَقَلْبُهُ مُطْمَئِنٌّ بِالْإِيمَانِ وَلَٰكِن مَّن
شَرَحَ بِالْكُفْرِ صَدْرًا فَعَلَيْهِمْ غَضَبٌ مِّنَ اللَّهِ وَلَهُمْ عَذَابٌ عَظِيمٌ"

"Whoever disbelieves in Allah after his belief except for one who is forced while his heart is secure in faith. But those who (willingly) open their hearts to disbelief, upon them is wrath from Allah, and for them is a great punishment."[201]

201 Q. (16:106).

HADITH 40

الحديث الأربعون

The Role of Man in This World

عن [ابنِ عمرَ] رَضِيَ اللهُ عَنْهُما قالَ: أَخَذَ رسولُ اللهِ صَلَّى اللهُ عَلَيْهِ وَسَلَّمَ بِمَنْكِبَيَّ فقالَ:
"كُنْ فِي الدُّنْيا كَأَنَّكَ غَرِيبٌ أَوْ عَابِرُ سَبِيلٍ". وكانَ ابنُ عُمَرَ رَضِيَ اللهُ عَنْهُما يقولُ: "إذا أمسيْتَ فلا تَنْتَظِرِ الصَّباحَ، وإذا أَصْبَحْتَ فَلا تَنْتَظِرِ المساءَ، وخُذْ مِن صِحَّتِكَ لِمَرَضِكَ، ومِنْ حياتِكَ لِمَوْتِكَ".
رواه البخاريُّ.

On the authority of ʿAbdullāh ibn ʿUmar (r.a.), who said,

The Messenger of Allah (peace and blessings of Allah be upon him) took me by the shoulder and said, "Be in this world as though you were a stranger or a wayfarer." And Ibn ʿUmar (r.a.) used to say, "In the evening do not expect (to live until) the morning, and in the morning do not expect (to live until) the evening. Take (advantage of) your health before times of sickness, and (take advantage of) your life before your death."

Related by al-Bukhārī.

Theme

- Viewing and living in this world as a temporary place

Explanation

To understand the meaning of this hadith, it is beneficial to begin with the interpretation provided by ʿAbdullāh ibn ʿUmar (r.a.), which holds great significance. He elucidates the prophetic hadith by describing the characteristics of the people whom the Prophet Muhammad (pbuh) refers to as travelers. His explanation highlights the sweetness of expressing and acting in accordance with the divine teachings that the Messenger of Allah (pbuh) has bequeathed to him and other companions.

At the outset, before advising Ibn ʿUmar, the Messenger of Allah (pbuh) takes hold of his arm, underscoring the importance of what he is about to say. The advice, "Be in this world as a stranger or a traveler," carries profound significance.

To be in this world as a stranger means to view the Hereafter as the ultimate destination where there is no death. Simultaneously, a person's actions and heart should align with Islamic divine teachings.

The reason for treating this world as temporary is that everything it offers is transient, whereas the offerings of the Hereafter are endless and eternal. Many of the material world's offerings distract a person from the remembrance of God and hinder their progress in doing good deeds. In fact, the material world, along with the whims and the accursed devil, are primary obstacles. Pursuing them creates a significant barrier between a person and their Creator.

However, through this hadith, the Messenger of Allah (pbuh) does not suggest that believers should completely detach themselves from this world to the extent of neglecting their own well-being or their responsibilities to themselves and others. Instead, they should take from this world what they need while remaining diligent in their religious and spiritual duties. Complete detachment can hinder many from fulfilling their obligations. As the elders often say, "O child! Let money enter your pocket, but not your heart."[202]

Regarding the reality of this world, Allah reminds people through the Qur'anic verses,

---

[202] This is a traditional Albanian saying.

"يَا أَيُّهَا النَّاسُ اتَّقُوا رَبَّكُمْ وَاخْشَوْا يَوْمًا لَّا يَجْزِي وَالِدٌ عَن وَلَدِهِ وَلَا مَوْلُودٌ هُوَ جَازٍ عَن وَالِدِهِ شَيْئًا إِنَّ وَعْدَ اللَّهِ حَقٌّ فَلَا تَغُرَّنَّكُمُ الْحَيَاةُ الدُّنْيَا وَلَا يَغُرَّنَّكُم بِاللَّهِ الْغَرُورُ"

"O humanity! Be mindful of your Lord, and beware of a Day when no parent will be of any benefit to their child, nor will a child be of any benefit to their parent. Surely Allah's promise is true. So do not let the life of this world deceive you, nor let the Chief Deceiver (Satan) deceive you about Allah."[203]

In another verse in the Noble Qur'an, Allah Almighty also says,

"اعْلَمُوا أَنَّمَا الْحَيَاةُ الدُّنْيَا لَعِبٌ وَلَهْوٌ وَزِينَةٌ وَتَفَاخُرٌ بَيْنَكُمْ وَتَكَاثُرٌ فِي الْأَمْوَالِ وَالْأَوْلَادِ كَمَثَلِ غَيْثٍ أَعْجَبَ الْكُفَّارَ نَبَاتُهُ ثُمَّ يَهِيجُ فَتَرَاهُ مُصْفَرًّا ثُمَّ يَكُونُ حُطَامًا وَفِي الْآخِرَةِ عَذَابٌ شَدِيدٌ وَمَغْفِرَةٌ مِّنَ اللَّهِ وَرِضْوَانٌ وَمَا الْحَيَاةُ الدُّنْيَا إِلَّا مَتَاعُ الْغُرُورِ"

"Know that the life of this world is but amusement and diversion and adornment and boasting to one another and competition in increase of wealth and children. It is like the example of rain whose (resulting) plant growth pleases the tillers; then it dries and you see it turned yellow; then it becomes (scattered) debris. And in the Hereafter is severe punishment and forgiveness from Allah and approval. And what is the worldly life except the enjoyment of delusion."[204]

In his book, *Al-Fatḥ al-Rabbānī*, the renowned scholar ʿAbd al-Qādir al-Jaylanī says,

---

[203] Q. (31:33).

[204] Q. (57:20).

O child! Give more importance to the life of the Hereafter than to the life of this world, and you will gain both. If you give more importance to the life of this world than to the Hereafter, as a punishment, you will lose both. You will be asked: "Why did you devote so much to something you were not advised to do?" If you do not spend your life in service to this material world, the Almighty God will grant you His support and assistance to overcome it, and then He will grant you success in obtaining your rightful share from it. Whatever you take from it will be blessed.[205]

The Sheikh then describes the snare of this world and the negative consequences if a person falls into its trap, "Your connection to this world has blinded your hearts to the point where you can no longer see anything. Beware of this world! It lures you to taste its pleasures occasionally, but then gradually leads you into its trap, capturing and fragmenting you. Initially, it allows you to drink from its intoxicating beverages, and under this influence, you rush to sever your hands, feet, and pluck your eyes from their sockets. When this numbing influence wears off and the time for awakening arrives, you will see the damage you have suffered. These are the consequences of loving this world, following desires, clinging tightly to it with your heart, and the enslavement it brings. This is its nature, so beware!?"[206]

The following story from Imam Ghazali's book *Mukāshafah al-Qulūb* illustrates the true value of this world. Once, Prophet ʿIsā (pbuh) was sitting with a man who was accompanying him. The man had three pieces of bread. After they ate two pieces, Prophet ʿIsā (pbuh) went to drink water from a nearby stream. When he returned, he noticed the third piece of bread was missing. He asked the man: "Who took the other piece of bread?" The man replied that he did not know.

They continued their journey and Prophet ʿIsā (pbuh) saw a gazelle with two fawns. He called one of the fawns, which approached Prophet

---

205 Abd al-Qadir al-Jaylani: *Al-Fath al-Rabbani wa al-Faydh al-Rahmani*, p. 63.
206 Ibid. p. 81.

ʿIsā (pbuh). He slaughtered it, and they both ate from its meat. After finishing the meat, Prophet ʿIsā (pbuh) commanded the fawn in the name of Allah to come back to life. And it did. Prophet ʿIsā (pbuh) told his companion, "I ask you in the name of the One who granted me the ability to perform this miracle, who ate the third piece of bread?" He replied that he did not know.

They continued their journey and reached a barren field. Prophet ʿIsā (pbuh) began to gather soil from the field and commanded it, by Allah's permission, to turn into gold. And it did. He divided the gold into three parts and then addressed his companion: "One-third is for me, one-third for you, and one-third for the one who ate the piece of bread." Upon hearing this, the companion confessed that he had eaten the last piece. Prophet ʿIsā (pbuh) told him to keep all the gold and left.

Meanwhile, two men saw all that wealth and decided to kill Prophet ʿIsā's (pbuh) companion and steal it. When they approached, the companion suggested, "Let's divide the wealth into three parts." The thieves agreed and sent one of them to the market to buy food. The man went and decided to poison the food to kill the other two and keep all the wealth for himself. At the same time, the two thieves planned to kill the man who would bring the food, so they could keep the wealth for themselves. And so they did.

When the man with the poisoned food arrived, they killed him and then, driven by hunger, began to eat the poisoned food and died as well. The barren field was left with gold and three dead bodies on it. Prophet cIsā (pbuh) passed by and, seeing them in this state, told his companions, "This is the material world, so beware!"[207]

In concluding the explanation of this hadith, it is fitting to mention a piece of Arabic poetry by the Islamic scholar Maḥmūd al-Bāhilī, whose verses draw inspiration from a prophetic hadith.

---

207 Abu Hamid Muhammad al-Ghazali: *Mukashafah al-Qulub*, translated from Arabic to English by Muhammad Muhammady, Dar al-Kutub al-Ilmiyya, Beirut, 2009, p. 351-2.

أَلَا إِنَّمَا الدُّنْيَا عَلَى الْمَرْءِ فِتْنَةٌ عَلَى كُلِّ حَالٍ أَقْبَلَتْ أَمْ تَوَلَّتْ

فَإِنْ أَقْبَلَتْ فَاسْتَقْبِلِ الشُّكْرَ دَائِمًا وَمَهْمَا تَوَلَّتْ فَاصْبِرْ وَثَبِّتْ

"Listen! This material world is a trial for humans,

It is a trial not only when it submits to them but also when it turns its back on them,

When it submits (to the believers), they should always be covered with gratitude,

And when it turns its back, they should endure and remain steadfast."[208]

[208] Al-Ghazali: *Mukashafah al-Qulub*, p. 354.

HADITH 41

الحديث الحادي والأربعون

Ambitions in Accordance with Divine Revelation

عَنْ أَبِي مُحَمَّدٍ عَبْدِ اللهِ بنِ عَمْرِو بنِ العاصِ رَضِيَ اللهُ عَنْهُما قالَ: قالَ رسولُ اللهِ صَلَّى اللهُ عَلَيْهِ وَسَلَّمَ:

"لاَ يُؤْمِنُ أَحَدُكُمْ حَتَّى يَكُونَ هَواهُ تَبَعًا لِمَا جِئْتُ بِهِ".

حديثٌ حسَنٌ صحيحٌ، رُوِّيناهُ في كتابِ الْحُجَّةِ بإسنادٍ صحيحٍ.

From Abū Muḥammad ʿAbd Allāh bin ʿAmr bin al-ʿĀṣ (r.a.) who said: The Messenger of Allah (pbuh) said,

"None of you truly believes until his inclination is in accordance with what I have brought."

(Imam al-Nawawī says,) "We have related it in *Kitāb al-Ḥujjah* with a sound chain of narrators."

Theme

- Attaining complete faith through following the prophetic example and renouncing desires

Explanation

One of life's greatest challenges is the battle against one's desires, a struggle commanded to be fought earnestly. These desires can hinder and lead one astray from the path of God. For example, some forsake prayer solely to gratify their desires, illustrating a prioritization of personal whims over divine commandments.

Although humans are honored creations of God, they can stoop to profound depths by indulging in their desires and following the accursed devil. The presence of challenges, desires, and the devil in one's life does not devalue them; rather, it illuminates and reveals the lofty virtues and benevolence bestowed by God upon them. Without evil, goodness would not only go unrecognized but would also lack the necessity of being achieved through diligence and sacrifice. Both diligence and sacrifice are crucial for attaining God's love and His rewards, both in this life and the Hereafter. Therefore, prioritizing His guidance over all else, including desires, is paramount because He is our Creator and possesses the supreme knowledge of the paths that lead us towards Him and His blessings.

In the Qur'an, numerous verses warn against following one's desires, emphasizing the repercussions of such actions. In Surah Al-Qaṣaṣ, Allah commands,

"وَمَنْ أَضَلُّ مِمَّنِ اتَّبَعَ هَوَاهُ بِغَيْرِ هُدًى مِّنَ اللَّهِ إِنَّ اللَّهَ لَا يَهْدِي الْقَوْمَ الظَّالِمِينَ"

"Who is more astray than one who follows his own desires without guidance from Allah? Truly, Allah does not guide wrongdoing people."[209]

Allah also promises Paradise to those who fear Him and restrain themselves from desires:

"وَأَمَّا مَنْ خَافَ مَقَامَ رَبِّهِ وَنَهَى النَّفْسَ عَنِ الْهَوَى. فَإِنَّ الْجَنَّةَ هِيَ الْمَأْوَى"

"But as for the one who feared standing before his Lord and restrained his soul from desires, then indeed, Paradise will be his refuge."[210]

Renouncing whims leads one closer to God. It is recounted that Prophet David (pbuh) once asked God, "O Lord, where can I find You?"

---

[209] Q. (28:50).

[210] Q. (79:40-1).

To which God replied, "Abandon your whims and draw near."[211] This exchange underscores whims as a barrier to divine proximity. When a person shields their heart from being consumed by worldly ambitions and attachments, nothing remains within it but Allah, enabling the servant's heart to reflect the Divine Presence. In this state, one diligently fulfills their Islamic obligations and maintains a steadfast connection with their Creator regardless of time or place. Ibn Ata'illāh al-Sakandarī (d. 709/1309), a revered Islamic scholar and author of *Al-Ḥikam*, remarked on whims, stating, "One of the signs of following whims is hastening to perform recommended (non-obligatory) deeds while being negligent in fulfilling obligatory ones."[212] In poetic verses, Imam Al-Shāfiʿī expressed,

تَعْصِي الإِلَهَ وَأَنْتَ تُظْهِرُ حُبَّهُ   هَذَا مَحَالٌ فِي القِيَاسِ بَدِيعُ

لَو كَانَ حُبُّكَ صَادِقًا لَأَطَعْتَهُ   إِنَّ المُحِبَّ لِمَنْ يُحِبُّ مُطِيعُ

"You disobey Allah while you outwardly show His love;
This is an impossible paradox in reasoning!

If your love were sincere, you would obey Him;
For the lover is obedient to the one he loves.[213]"

---

[211] Ahmad Ibn Ajiba al-Hasani: *Iqadh al-Himam fi Sharh al-Hikam*, Dar al-Ma'arif, Cairo, 2007, p. 422.

[212] Ibid.

[213] Muhammad Bin Idris Al-Shai'i: *Diwan al-Shafi'i*, Maktabah Al-Kulliyyat al-Azhariyyah, Cairo, 1985, p. 91.

HADITH 42

الحديث الثاني والأربعون

Allah's Forgiveness for the Repentant

عَنْ أَنَسٍ رَضِيَ اللهُ عَنْهُ قال: سَمِعْتُ رَسُولَ اللهِ صَلَّى اللهُ عَلَيْهِ وَسَلَّمَ يقولُ: "قَالَ اللهُ تَعَالَى: يَا ابْنَ آدَمَ، إِنَّكَ مَا دَعَوْتَنِي وَرَجَوْتَنِي غَفَرْتُ لَكَ عَلَى مَا كَانَ مِنْكَ وَلاَ أُبَالِي، يَا ابْنَ آدَمَ، لَوْ بَلَغَتْ ذُنُوبُكَ عَنَانَ السَّمَاءِ ثُمَّ اسْتَغْفَرْتَنِي غَفَرْتُ لَكَ، يَا ابْنَ آدَمَ، إِنَّكَ لَوْ أَتَيْتَنِي بِقُرَابِ الأَرْضِ خَطَايَا ثُمَّ لَقِيتَنِي لاَ تُشْرِكُ بِي شَيْئًا لأَتَيْتُكَ بِقُرَابِهَا مَغْفِرَةً".

رواهُ التِّرْمِذيُّ، وقالَ: حديثٌ حَسَنٌ صحيح.

On the authority of Anas (r.a.) who said: I heard the Messenger of Allah (pbuh) say,

"Allah the Almighty has said, 'O Son of Adam, as long as you invoke Me and ask of Me, I shall forgive you for what you have done, and I shall not mind. O Son of Adam, were your sins to reach the clouds of the sky and you then asked forgiveness from Me, I would forgive you. O Son of Adam, were you to come to Me with sins nearly as great as the Earth, and were you then to face Me, ascribing no partner to Me, I would bring you forgiveness nearly as great as it (too).'"

Related by al-Tirmidhī, who said that it was a reliable-sound hadith.

Themes

- God's forgiveness surpasses human sins
- Connection with God through prayer, hope, and forgiveness

Explanation

Imam al-Nawawī placed the above hadith at the end of his book because it encompasses the theme of divine forgiveness, a central element in Islam. Seeking and achieving divine forgiveness should be a daily spiritual practice. Those who have lived a life contrary to divine teachings and seek forgiveness only when death approaches, their repentance will not be accepted. As stated in the Qur'an,

"إِنَّمَا التَّوْبَةُ عَلَى اللَّهِ لِلَّذِينَ يَعْمَلُونَ السُّوءَ بِجَهَالَةٍ ثُمَّ يَتُوبُونَ مِن قَرِيبٍ فَأُولَئِكَ يَتُوبُ اللَّهُ عَلَيْهِمْ وَكَانَ اللَّهُ عَلِيمًا حَكِيمًا. وَلَيْسَتِ التَّوْبَةُ لِلَّذِينَ يَعْمَلُونَ السَّيِّئَاتِ حَتَّى إِذَا حَضَرَ أَحَدَهُمُ الْمَوْتُ قَالَ إِنِّي تُبْتُ الْآنَ وَلَا الَّذِينَ يَمُوتُونَ وَهُمْ كُفَّارٌ أُولَئِكَ أَعْتَدْنَا لَهُمْ عَذَابًا أَلِيمًا"

"Allah accepts the repentance of those who do evil in ignorance and repent soon after. To them, Allah will turn in mercy. Allah is Knowing and Wise. But repentance is not for those who continue to do evil deeds until death comes to one of them and he says, 'Indeed, I have repented now,' or of those who die while they are disbelievers. For them, We have prepared a painful punishment."[214]

Another essential aspect is that people should not expect Allah to forgive their sins if they have wronged others. They must reconcile with those they have wronged and seek forgiveness from them before asking for Allah's forgiveness.

Praying to God for forgiveness strengthens a person's connection with their Creator and makes them humbler before Him. People who do not seek forgiveness for their mistakes are often arrogant.

---

[214] Q. (4:17-18).

When a person sincerely prays to God for forgiveness, two profound phenomena occur: the recognition of Allah as the true God and the affirmation of belief in Him. This belief is expressed through the person's hope, trusting that Allah is the One who forgives sins and earnestly hoping for His forgiveness. Conversely, Allah's mercy and presence are revealed to the person through His divine attribute of forgiveness. One of His beautiful names, by which He wishes to be known and invoked, is "The Great Forgiver" (*Al-Ghaffār*).[215]

Even though a person may be burdened with sins, they must never lose hope in God. Losing hope signifies a broken connection between the creature and the Creator, while praying for forgiveness and turning to Him demonstrates the preservation of this divine connection.

From oral traditions it is mentioned that once, a person was seen robbing in the market. Later, to the observer's surprise, the robber joined the congregational prayer. After the prayer, the observer confronted the robber, asking how he could reconcile his actions. The robber replied, "Despite my many sins, I am sure I have lost many of God's blessings, but I hope that through prayer, I do not sever my connection with Him completely."

The beginning of this hadith carries profound significance, where the Almighty Allah addresses not just the believers but all of humanity by saying, "O son of Adam!" This indicates that Allah, being the God of all mankind, invites everyone to turn to Him with prayer and hope.

Reflecting on the first part of this hadith where it mentions, "As long as you call upon Me and hope in Me, I will forgive you for what you have done," one understands that every prayer directed to Him, or even the mere hope in Him, may lead to the forgiveness of sins. However, this does not mean that one who lives a righteous life should neglect seeking forgiveness. The act of seeking forgiveness itself, aside from its other benefits, aids in abandoning sin, and no one is immune to it except Prophets and Messengers of God. The Messenger of Allah (pbuh), despite his elevated status with God and his already forgiven sins, regularly sought forgiveness from God every day.

---

[215] For more on this topic, you can read the explanation of Hadith 24 in this book.

According to prophetic traditions, the most preferred prayer for forgiveness of sins is,

"اللّهمَّ أَنْتَ رَبِّي لا إلهَ إلاّ أَنْتَ خَلَقْتَني وَأَنا عَبْدُك وَأنا على عَهْدِكَ وَوَعْدِكَ ما اسْتَطَعْتُ أَعوذُ بِكَ مِنْ شَرِّ ما صَنَعْتُ أَبوءُ لَكَ بِنِعْمَتِكَ عَلَيَّ وَأَبوءُ بِذَنْبي فَاغْفِرْ لي فَإِنَّهُ لا يَغْفِرُ الذُّنوبَ إِلاّ أَنْتَ".

"O Allah, You are my Lord, there is no deity but You. You created me, and I am Your servant, and I will remain faithful to Your covenant and promise as much as I can. I seek refuge in You from the evil I have done. I am grateful for Your blessings upon me. I acknowledge my sins, so forgive me, for no one can forgive sins except You."[216]

In the same hadith, the Messenger of Allah (pbuh) mentions that a believer who says this during the day and dies before evening will enter Paradise, and if they say it in the evening and die before morning, they will enter Paradise.[217]

In Arabic, there are two words often used in seeking forgiveness from God: "*istighfār*" and "*tawbah*." The word *istighfār* means praying for the forgiveness of sins, while the word *tawbah* means returning, which implies repentance. The concept of *tawbah* is connected to the idea that a person is created with a pure nature, inclined towards good deeds. Over time, sins and external influences may divert them from the right path. When people repent and cease committing sins, they essentially return to their original, pure nature. This return to one's innate state of purity is a fundamental aspect of the meaning of *tawbah*.

According to Imam Ibn Rajab, one of the most crucial conditions for the acceptance of repentance is that the person feels it sincerely in their heart when seeking forgiveness from God.[218] Abu Hurayrah (r.a.) narrates a hadith of the Messenger of Allah (pbuh) where he instructs people, saying,

---

[216] Al-Bukhārī: *Sahih al-Bukhari bi Sharh al-Kirmani*, vol. 22, p. 124.

[217] Ibid.

[218] Zayn al-Din ibn Shihab al-Din: *Jami' al-Ulum wa al-Hikam*, p. 832.

"ادْعُوا اللَّهَ وَأَنْتُمْ مُوقِنُونَ بِالْإِجَابَةِ وَاعْلَمُوا أَنَّ اللَّهَ لَا يَسْتَجِيبُ دُعَاءً مِنْ قَلْبٍ غَافِلٍ لَاهٍ"

"Pray to God in a way that deserves a response from Him, and know that Allah does not respond to a prayer that comes from a careless and inattentive heart."[219]

Additionally, it is important that when seeking forgiveness and turning to God, the person does not repeat the same sin. Otherwise, their act of seeking forgiveness reveals a lack of sincerity. Imam Ibn Rajab also cites a pious individual's saying: "If seeking forgiveness does not lead to the perfection of repentance, then the person is not sincere in seeking forgiveness." Similarly, the Islamic mystic scholar Dhu Al-Nūn al-Miṣrī states, "Seeking forgiveness without avoiding sin is the repentance of liars."[220]

---

219 Muhammad ibn Ja'qub Kalabadhi: *Bahr al-Fawa'id*, Dar al-Kutub al-Ilmiyyah, Beirut, 1999, p. 32.

220 Farid al-Din ʿAttar, *Memorial of God's Friends*, translated by Paul Losensky, Paulist Press, New Jersey, 2009, p. 175.

And Allah is the Helper in granting success.

وَاللهُ وَلِيُّ التَّوْفِيقِ

Glossary

ahl al-baqā'	people who have attained a deep knowledge of Allah and await manifestations
ahl al-bayt	the Prophet's (pbuh) family
ahl al-fanā'	people who have attained a deep knowledge of Allah and are immersed in His love
ahl al-ṣuffa	"People of the Bench"; known for their profound love for the Messenger of Allah (pbuh)
ᶜalāmāt al-sā'ah	Signs of the Day of Judgment
Allahu Akbar	God is greater
arkān al-īmān	foundations of faith
asānīd	chains of narration
asbāb al-nuzūl	reasons behind the revelations
Ash-hadu an lā ilāha il-lallāh, wa ash-hadu anna Muhammadan ᶜabduhu wa rasūluhu	I declare there is no god but Allah, and I declare that Muhammad is the Messenger of Allah and His servant

awliyā' Allāh	close servants of God
Ayah	verse in the Qur'an
bid^cah	innovation
bid^cah ḥasanah	good innovation
bid^cah lughawiyyah	linguistic innovation
bid^cah qabīḥah	bad innovation
al-birr	good morality; purity from sins
burhān	proof
ḍa'īf	weak
ḍarar	harm
al-ḍarūriy-yāt al-khams	five essential principles (to be preserved by sharia)
dhikr	remembrance of Allah
dīn	religion
ḍirār	to harm
ḍiyā'	radiant light
Duḥā	supererogatory prayer in the morning, after the sun rises.
farā'id	religious obligations
fatwa	non-binding Islamic legal opinions
fiqh	Islamic Jurisprudence
Al-Ghaffār	The Great Forgiver
ghusl	ritual ablution to cleanse the whole body with clean water

hadith	lit. "event" or "news"; narration of the words, deeds, reports, and qualities of Prophet Muhammad (pbuh)
ḥajj	pilgrimage
al-ḥamd	gratitude to God
Al-ḥamdu lil-lāh	praise be to Allah
ḥaqīqah	divine reality
harām	prohibited
ḥayā'	modesty; sensitivity
ḥasad	envy
ḥasan	good
al-hidāyah	guidance
hijrah	migration
ḥub	love
ḥudūd	punishments
ḥusn al-khuluq	good conduct
Iblīs	Satan
al-ᶜiffah	chastity
iftar	meal to break a fast
iḥsān	worship
ijāzah	license, certification (of Islamic knowledge)
ijtihād	efforts
ikhlāṣ	sincerity

al-īmān	faith
Islām	lit. "surrendering"; pertains to the practical pillars of the faith
isnād	line of transmission
al-Istiqāmah	Steadfastness
istighfār	praying for the forgiveness of sins
al-īthār	altruism
Jibrīl	Gabriel
jihād	striving in the path of God
jinn	non-human beings made by God that cannot be seen but interact with humans
karāmāt	miracles
al-khaṭa'	mistake
Lā ilāha il-lāll-llāh	there is no god except Allah
Lawḥ al-Maḥfūdh	Preserved Tablet, where the entire Qur'an was recorded before Archangel Gabriel conveyed it to Prophet Muhammad (pbuh), and contains undisclosed information about humanity
Laylat al-Qadr	Night of Decree
madrasah	school
maḥabbah	love
al-mahdiyyīn	those on the right path
maḥfūẓ	protected

maqām	favorable state
ma'ṣūm	infallible
al-mīzān	the scale good deeds
mubāh	permissible
mudda^cī	plaintiff
muhājir	emigrant
mursal	"sent or transmitted," a hadith narrated by a companion of the Prophet (pbuh) who did not hear it directly from the Prophet (pbuh) himself
mushtabihāt	doubtful matters
nāfilah	supererogatory
Nafs	ego
al-najsh	deceit in trade
al-nās	people (can refer to all people, specific individuals, or social groups)
naṣīḥah	advice; sincerity
niyyah	intention
niṣāb	minimum threshold of wealth that makes zakāt mandatory
nūr	light (of the moon)
qaḍā	divine will
qadar	destiny, divine decree
qalb	metaphysical heart

qitāl	fighting
Qudsi	a type of hadith in which the Prophet (pbuh) is transmitting words or meanings from God. These are not in the Qur'an, and the only exception to exact transmission is when the Prophet (pbuh) describes God
rakʿah	unit of prayer
al-rashidūn	rightly guided
ṣabr	patience
ṣabr ʿalā fuḍūl al-dunyā	patience in avoiding excessive and unnecessary worldly matters
ṣabr ʿalā maṣāʾib al-dunyā	patience in facing worldly trials
ṣabr ʿalā al-maʿṣiyah	patience in abstaining from sins
ṣabr ʿalā al-ṭāʿah	patience in obedience to Allah
ṣadaqah	charity
ṣaḥīḥ	authentic
sakīnah	tranquility
ṣalat	prayer
sawm	fasting
shahādah	Declaration of Faith
sharia	Islamic law
shirk	worshiping any deity other than Allah
subḥān-Allah	how far from imperfection is Allah

subḥān Allāh wa al- ḥamdu li-llāh	praise and thanks belong to Allah
sunnah	prophetic tradition
sunnah sayyiah	bad practice
Surah	chapter of the Qur'an
al-ṭāᶜah	obedience to Allah
tābi 'īn	the generation immediately following the Prophet's companions (may God be pleased with them all)
tābi ' al-tābi 'īn	the third generation following the Prophet's companions (may God be pleased with them all)
tafsīr	Qur'anic Exegesis
tahlīl	declaration of Allah's Oneness; saying *Lā Ilāha il-lā Allāh*
taḥmīd	praise of Allah; saying *al-ḥamdulil-lāh*
tāj al-ᶜārifīn	crown of the gnostics
tajwīd	rules of reading
takbīr	exaltation of Allah; saying *Allahu Akbar*
ṭalāq	divorce
taqwa	piety; fear of Allah
ṭarīq	the path
tasbih	glorification of Allah; saying *subḥān Allāh*

tawbah	repentance; returning to one's innate state of purity
tawḥīd	the Unity and Oneness of Allah
tayammum	ritual ablution to cleanse the face and hands with soil
tazkiyah	self-purification
uṣūl al-hadīth	Principles of Hadith
uṣūl al-fiqh	Islamic Legal Principles
uṣūl al-tafsīr	Principles of Qur'anic Interpretation
wilāyah al-ʻāmmah	all those who possess faith and devotion to Allah
wilāyah al-khāṣṣah	those who have attained deep knowledge of Allah, are immersed in His love, and await divine manifestations
waliyy	friend; plural: ***awliyā'***
zakāt	charity, almsgiving
zuhd	asceticism

Bibliography

Abū Dāwūd al-Sijistānī. *Sunan Abī Dāwūd.* 7 vols. Dār al-Risālah al-ʿĀlamiyyah, Damascus, 2009.

Abī al-Dunyā, Ibn. *Makārim al-Akhlāq*. Maktabah al-Qurʾān, Cairo, 1990.

Abū Dāwūd al-Sijistānī. *Sunan Abī Dāwūd.* 7 vols. Dār al-Risālah al-ʿĀlamiyyah, Damascus, 2009.

al-Asqalānī, Muḥammad Ibn Ḥajar. *Fatḥ al-Bārī Sharḥ Ṣaḥīḥ* al-*Bukhārī.* 13 vols. Dār al-Rayyān, Cairo, 1986.

al-Asqalānī, Muḥammad Ibn Ḥajar. *Fatḥ al-Bārī.* 14 vols. Iḥyāʾ al-Turāth al-ʿArabī, Beirut, 1981.

al-Aṭṭār, ʿAlāʾ al-Dīn ʿAlī. *Tuhfat al- Ṭālibīn fī Tarjamat al-Imām al-Nawawī.* Dār al-Athariyyah, Amman, 2007.

al-Baghdādī, Abū al-Qāsim Ibn Bishrān. *Amālī Ibn Bishrān.* Dār al-Waṭan, Riyadh, 1997.

al-Bayhaqī, Abū Bakr Aḥmad Ibn al-Ḥusayn. *Al-Jāmiʿ li Shuʿab al-*Īmān. Maktabat al-Rushd, Riyadh, 2003.

al-Bayhaqī, Abū Bakr Aḥmad Ibn al-Ḥusayn. *Kitāb al-Zuhd al-Kabīr.* 1st ed. Dār al-Khinān, Beirut, 1987.

al-Bughā, Dr. Muṣtafā and Mistū, Muḥyiddīn. *Al-Wāfī fī Sharḥ al-Arbaʿīn al-Nawawiyya.* Damascus, no publishing year available.

al-Bukhārī, Muḥammad Ibn Ismā'īl. *Al-Kawākib al-Darārī fī Sharḥ Ṣaḥīḥ* al-*Bukhārī*. Dār Iḥyā' al-Turāth al-'Arabī, Beirut, 2nd ed., 1981.

al-Bukhārī, Muḥammad Ibn Ismā'īl. *Book of Muslim's Moral and Manners*. Translated from Arabic into English by Yusuf Talal DeLorenzo. Al-Saadawi Publications, Alexandria, USA, 1999.

al-Ḥanafī, Badr al-Dīn al-'Aynī. *Al-Bināya Sharḥ al-Hidāya*. Dār al-Kutub al-'Ilmiyyah, Beirut, 2000.

al-Ḥanbalī, Aḥmad Ibn Ḥanbal. *Musnad Aḥmad Ibn Ḥanbal*. Dār al-Ḥadīth, Cairo, 1995.

al-Ḥasanī, Aḥmad Ibn 'Ajībah. *Al-Baḥr al-Madīd fī Tafsīr al-Qur'ān al-Majīd*. 8 vols. Dār al-Kutub al-'Ilmiyyah, Beirut. 2010.

al-Ḥasanī, Aḥmad Ibn 'Ajībah. *Iqāẓ* al-*Himam fī Sharḥ al-Ḥikam*. Dār al-Ma'ārif, Cairo, 2007.

al-Ḥujwīrī, 'Alī bin 'Uthmān. *Kashf al-Maḥjūb*. Translated from Persian to English by Reynold A. Nicholson. E.J.W. GIBB Memorial Trust, Wiltshire, England, 2000.

al-'Īd, Ibn Daqīq. *"A Treasury of Hadith: A Commentary on Nawawi's Selection of Forty Prophetic Traditions."* Translated by Mokrane Guezzou. Leicestershire, UK: Kube Publishing, 2016.

al-Jawziyyah, Ibn al-Qayyim. *Zād al-Ma'ād fī Hadī Khayr al-*'Ibād. Mu'assasat al-Risālah, Beirut, 1994.

al-Jawziyyah, Muḥammad ibn al-Qayyim. *Al-Jawāb al-Kāfī liman Sa'ala* 'an *al-Dawā' al-Shāfī*. Dār al-Ma'rifah, Beirut, 1997.

al-Jaylānī, 'Abd al-Qādir. *Al-Fatḥ al-Rabbānī wa al-Fayḍ al-Raḥmānī*. Dār al-Albāb, Beirut. (no publishing year available).

Al-Jurjani, Abu Bakr. *The Wisdom of the Sufis: Collection of Mystical Sayings*. Translated by A. Ezzati. Oxford: OneWorld Publications, 1996.

al-Kalābādhī, Abū Bakr. *Al-Ta'arruf li Madhhab Ahl al-Taṣawwuf*. Dār al-Kutub al-'Ilmiyyah, Beirut, 1993.

al-Kalābādhī, Muḥammad Ibn Yaʿqūb. *Baḥr al-Fawāʾid.* Dār al-Kutub al-ʿIlmiyya, Beirut, 1999.

al-Maḥallī, Jalāl al-Dīn, and al-Suyūṭī, Jalāl al-Dīn. *Tafsīr al-Jalālayn.* al-Maktab al-Islāmī, Beirut, special edition by the Ministry of Religion for Islamic Affairs of the State of Qatar, (year missing).

al-Mālikī, Ibn Anas. *Al-Muwaṭṭaʾ.* Dār al-Turāth al-ʿArabī, Beirut, 1985.

al-Maqdisī, Muḥammad Ibn Mufliḥ. *Al-Adab al-Sharʿiyyah.* Muʾassasat al-Risālah, 3rd ed., Beirut, 1999.

al-Maqrīzī, Aḥmad Ibn ʿAlī Ibn ʿAbd al-Qādir. *Iqāẓ al-Himam.* Dār al-Maʿārif, Cairo, 2007.

al-Mūṣalī, Abū Yaʿlā. *Musnad Abī Yaʿlā al-Mūṣalī.* 16 vols. Dār al-Maʾmūn li al-Turāth, Damascus, 1989.

al-Naqshbandī, Amīn ʿAlāʾ al-Dīn. *Sufism: A Wayfarer's Guide to the Naqshbandī Way.* Translated from Arabic to English by Muhtar Holland, Louisville, 2011.

al-Nasāʾī, Abū ʿAbd al-Raḥmān. *Musnad al-Nasāʾī al-Mujtabā.* 9 vols. Dār al-Risālah al-ʿĀlamiyyah, Riyadh, 2018.

al-Nawawī, Abū Zakariyyā. *Al-Minhāj fī Sharḥ Ṣaḥīḥ Muslim bin al-Ḥajjāj.* Bayt al-Afkār al-Dawliyyah, Riyadh.

al-Nawawī, Abū Zakariyyā. *Tahdhīb al-Asmāʾ wa al-Lughāt.* 4 vols. Dār al-Kutub al-ʿIlmiyya, Beirut. (no publishing year available).

al-Naysābūrī, Abū ʿAbdillah al-Ḥakīm. *Al-Mustadrak* ʿalā *al-Ṣaḥīḥayn.* Dār al-Ḥaramayn, Cairo, 1997.

al-Qazwīnī, Muḥammad Ibn Yazīd Ibn Mājah. *Sunan Ibn Mājah.* 5 vols. Dār al-Risālah al-ʿĀlamiyyah, Damascus, 2009.

al-Qurtubī, Muḥammad Ibn Aḥmad Ibn Abī Bakr. *Jāmiʿ al-Aḥkām al-Qurʾān.* 24 vols. Muʾassasat al-Risālah Nashirūn, Damascus, 2006.

al-Qushayrī, Abū al-Qāsim. *Al-Risāla al-Qushayriyya.* Maṭba'Mu'assasah Dār al-Sha'b, Cairo, 1989.

al-Qushayrī, Abū al-Qāsim. *Laṭā'if al-Ishārāt.* 3 vols. Dār al-Kutub al-'Ilmiyyah, Beirut, 2000.

al-Raysūnī, Aḥmad. *Naẓariyyāt al-Maqāṣid* 'ind *al-Imām al-Shāṭibī.* Al-Majid al-'Ālamī li al-Fikr al-Islāmī.

al-Rāzī, Abū 'Abdullah. *Mashyakhah Abī* 'Abdullāh *al-Rāzī.* Dār al-Hijrah, Riyadh, 1994.

al-Sakhāwī, Shams al-Dīn. *Al-Manhal al-*'Adhb *fī Tarjamat Quṭb al-Awliyā' al-Nawawī.* Dār al-Kutub al-'Ilmiyyah, Beirut, 2005.

al-Sarrāj, Abū Naṣr. *Kitāb Luma'.* Dār al-Kutub al-Ḥadītha bi Miṣr, Cairo, 1987.

al-Shafi'ī, Muḥammad bin Idrīs. *Diwān al-Shafi*'ī. Cairo: Maktabah Al-Kulliyyāt al-Azhariyyah, 1985.

al-Sha'ranī, 'Abd al-Wahhāb Ibn Aḥmad. *Al-Yawāqīt wa al-Jawāhir fī Bayān* 'Aqā'id *al-Akābir.* 2 vols. Dār al-Kutub al-'Ilmiyyah, Beirut, 2001.

al-Shāmī, Muḥammad. *Subul al-Hudā wa al-Rashād.* 12 vols. Dār al-Kutub al-'Ilmiyya, Beirut, 1993.

al-Suyūṭī, Jalāl al-Dīn. *Al-Durr al-Manthūr fī Tafsīr al-Ma'thūr.* 8 vols. Dār al-Fikr, Beirut, 1993.

al-Ṭabarānī, Ibn Aḥmad Sulaymān. *Al-Mu'jam al-Awṣaṭ.* Dār al-Ḥaramayn, Cairo, 1995.

al-Ṭabarī, Muḥammad Ibn Jarīr. *Tafsīr al-Ṭabarī.* Dār al-Kutub al-'Ilmiyyah, Beirut, 2001.

al-Taftāzānī, Sa'd al-Dīn Maḥmūd ibn 'Umar ibn 'Abdallāh. *Sharḥ al-Taftāzānī* 'alā *al-Arba'īn al-Nawawiyya.* Dār al-Kutub

al-'Ilmiyyah, Beirut, 2004.

al-Tirmidhī, Muḥammad ibn ʿĪsā. *Al-Jāmiʿ al-Ṣaḥīḥ*. 6 vols. Maktabah wa Maṭbaʿah Muṣṯafā al-Bābī al-Ḥalabī wa Awlāduh, 1st ed., Cairo, 1962.

al-Tirmidhī, Muḥammad Ibn ʿĪsā. *Jāmiʿ al-Tirmidhī*. 6 vols. Dār al-Kutub al-ʿIlmiyyah, Beirut, 1998.

al-Tirmidhī, Muḥammad ibn ʿĪsā. *Shamāʾil al-Nabī*. Dār al-Gharb al-Islāmī, Beirut, 2000.

al-Zamakhsharī, Maḥmūd Ibn ʿUmar. *Al-Kashshāf*. Dār al-Maʿārif, Cairo, 1987.

al-Zarrūq, Aḥmad ibn Muḥammad. *al-Nāṣīḥah al-Kāfiyah*. Maktabat al-Imām al-Shāfiʿī, 1st ed., Riyadh, 1993.

al-ʿAsqalānī, Ibn Ḥajar. *Sharḥ al-Arbaʿīn ḥadīthan al-Nawawiyyah*, with notes from Riyāḍ ʿĪsā Manṣī and ʿAbd al-Qādir Muṣṯafā Ṭāhā. 1st edition, Jordan, 2013.

Ata Alsid, Sidahmad. *The Hudud*. Al-Basheer Publication, Malaysia, 1995.

Aṭṭār, Farīd al-Dīn. *Memorial of God's Friends*. Translated into English by Paul Losensky. Paulist Press, New Jersey, 2009.

Bin Shihāb al-Dīn, Zayn al-Dīn. *Jāmiʿ al-*ʿUlūm *wa al-Ḥikam*. Dār Ibn Kathīr, Damascus, 2008.

Dalliu, Ibrahim. *Me shënimet: Hadíthi – Errbeàín, Dyzet fjalë përmbledhse të Pejgamberit, alejhisselam të cilat i bâhen udhëheqse e plotsimit të* çdo *myslimani si kah besimi ashtû edhe kah moralet dhe kah veprat. Përmbledhë prej Imami Muhjiddini Neveviut.* Translated from Arabic to Albanian by Hafiz Ibrahim Dalliu. Given for free. Tiranë, Publishing House Shkodra, 1934.

Davis, Tchiki. "Managing Anger: Tips, Techniques, and Tools." *Psychology Today*. Accessed October 12, 2024. https://www.psychologytoday.com/us/blog/click-here-happiness/202203/managing-anger-tips-techniques-and-tools.

Fili, Burhan Al-Din S. *Katërdhet hadithe (Fjalë të profetit Muhammed A.S.) Zgjedhun prej: Imam Sherefed-din Neveviut.* Translated and added notes by Burhan Al-Din S. Fili. First Published in 1986, Albanian Islamic Center Harper Wood, MI, 1986.

Ghazālī, Abū Ḥāmid. *Iḥyā'* 'Ulūm *al-Dīn.* 4 vols. Dār al-Ma'rifah, Beirut, 1982.

Ghazālī, Abū Ḥāmid. *Minhāj al-'*Ābidīn. Mu'assasat al-Risālah, 1st ed., Beirut, 1989.

Ghazālī, Abū Ḥāmid. *Mukāshafah al-Qulūb.* Translated from Arabic to English by Muhammad Muhammady. Dār al-Kutub al-'Ilmiyyah, Beirut, 2009.

Hāshim, Aḥmad 'Umar. *Qawā'id Usūl al-Ḥadīth.* Dār al-Kutub al-'Arabī, Beirut, 1984.

Ibn Abī Bakr, Muḥammad (known as Ibn al-Qayyim al-Jawziyya). *Al-Jawāb al-Kāfi liman Sa'ala* 'an *al-Dawā' al-Shāfi.* Dār al-Ma'rifah, Beirut, 1997.

Ibn al-Ḥajjāj, Muslim. *Ṣaḥīḥ* Muslim. 2 vols. Dār al-Ṭayyibah, Riyadh, 2006.

Ibn Ḥibbān, Muḥammad. *Ṣaḥīḥ* Ibn *Ḥibbān.* 8 vols. Dār Ibn Ḥazm, Beirut, 2012.

Ibn Khuzaymah, Muḥammad. *Ṣaḥīḥ* Ibn Khuzaymah. 4 vols. al-Maktab al-Islāmī, Beirut, 1970.

Ibn Taymiyyah, Taqī al-Dīn Aḥmad. *Iqtiḍā' Ṣirāṭ al-Mustaqīm.* 2 vols. Maktabah al-Rushd, Riyadh, 2006.

Ismaili, Vehbi. *Kolana e veprave të Imam Vehbi Ismaili.* Work 6, LOGOS-A, Skopje, 2009.

Mar'ī, Kamāl Ḥasan. *Al-Majmu' al-Kabīr min al-Mutūn fimā yudhkar min al-Funūn.* 2 vols. Al-Maktabah al-'Aṣriyyah, Beirut, 2005.

Shāfī, Muḥammad. *Ma'ariful Qur'an: A Comprehensive Commentary on the Holy Quran*. Karachi: Maktaba-e-Darul-Uloom, 2020.

World Cancer Research Fund International. "Ultra-processed Foods Linked to Increased Cancer Risk, Diabetes, and Heart Disease." November 14, 2023. https://www.wcrf.org/news-events/ultra-processed-foods-linked-to-increased-cancer-risk-diabetes-and-heart-disease.

About the Author

Didmar Faja is the Imam of the United Islamic Center of Arizona (UICA) in Glendale, Arizona, and the founder and President of Greenway Academy. Additionally, he has established two Islamic centers in Mexico. He serves as a religious advisor for the Naqshbandiyya Foundation for Islamic Education and teaches at the Madina Institute USA. Imam Didmar also heads the Imams Council of Arizona.

He received his early education in Shkodër, Albania, and completed his Islamic studies in Istanbul, Turkey. After moving to the US, he earned a Bachelor's degree in Islamic Studies and a Master of Divinity in Islamic Chaplaincy. Imam Didmar has studied under various scholars and holds traditional licenses (*ijāzāt*) to teach in several Islamic disciplines, including the issuance of non-binding Islamic opinions (*fatāwā*).

Made in the USA
Middletown, DE
17 January 2025

68837048R00119